YOU CAN HAVE AN
AMAZING
MEMORY

Dominic O'Brien is renowned for his phenomenal feats of memory and for outwitting the casinos of Las Vegas at the blackjack tables, resulting in a ban. In addition to winning the World Memory Championships eight times, he was named the Brain Trust of Great Britain's Brain of the Year in 1994 and Grandmaster of Memory in 1995. He has made numerous appearances on TV and radio and holds a host of world records, including one for memorizing 2,385 random binary digits in 30 minutes. In 2005 he was given a lifetime achievement award by the World Memory Championships International in recognition of his work to promote the art of memory all over the world; and in 2010 he became the General Manager of the World Memory Sports Council.

By the same author (all published by Duncan Baird Publishers)

How to Develop a Brilliant Memory: Week by Week
How to Pass Exams
Learn to Remember
Never Forget: A Name or Face
Never Forget: A Number or Date

YOU CAN HAVE AN AMAZING MEMORY

Learn life-changing techniques and tips from the memory maestro

DOMINIC O'BRIEN
Eight Times World Memory Champion

WATKINS PUBLISHING

LONDON

Distributed in the USA and Canada by Sterling Publishing Co., Inc.
387 Park Avenue South, New York, NY 10016-8810

This edition published in the UK and USA in 2011 by
Watkins Publishing, Sixth Floor, Castle House,
75–76 Wells Street, London W1T 3QH

1 3 5 7 9 10 8 6 4 2

Designed and typeset by Luana Gobbo
Edited by Judy Barratt

Printed and bound in India by Imago

Library of Congress Cataloging-in-Publication Data Available

ISBN: 978-1-907486-45-6

www.watkinspublishing.co.uk

For information about custom editions, special sales, premium and
corporate purchases, please contact Sterling Special Sales
Department at 800-805-5489 or specialsales@sterlingpub.com

CONTENTS

"The mind is like a trunk: if well-packed, it holds almost every thing; if ill-packed, next to nothing."

Augustus William Hare and Julius Charles Hare
Guesses at Truth, by Two Brothers, 1827

FOREWORD

As a child I was diagnosed with dyslexia and I was told by my form teacher at school that I would not amount to much in life. In fact, throughout my school days, no one held out much hope for me. Certainly, no one entertained the thought that one day I'd appear in the *Guinness World Records* book for what others have described as a feat of staggering brain power, or that I'd become World Memory Champion, not just once but eight times over! Here are some of the comments from my school reports when I was aged ten – they make unhappy reading:

"He tends to dream in the middle of a calculation, which leads him to lose track of the thought."

"[Dominic] has not paid much attention. Appears to know more of the Universe than the Earth."

"Terribly slow. Often cannot repeat the question. Must concentrate."

"Unless Dominic really shakes himself up and gets down to work, he is not going to achieve any success ... he is painfully slow."

Although they might sound harsh, these reports paint a fairly accurate picture of my state of mind as a child. I felt as though my brain was like a muscle that was permanently relaxed. My teachers knew it, and they were endlessly frustrated with me. In those days, teachers weren't governed by quite the same codes of conduct they are today, and one in particular behaved appallingly toward me – shaking me, shouting at me and generally humiliating me in front of my friends. I guess he hoped to bring me out of my apparent stupor.

Needless to say, I became highly stressed about going to school. In fact, I was completely terrified. By the age of 11, I hated it, but not only that – I was also emptied of all self-esteem. I regret to say that walking out through the school gates at the earliest possible opportunity felt (at the time, at least) like one of the happiest days of my life.

Almost 15 years later, I taught myself to memorize a deck of cards. I can't describe to you how that felt – not only had I achieved an amazing feat of mental agility, I had also made a symbolic conquest. I had kicked back at all the mistreatment, negativity and bad reports I'd received in my youth. I suddenly realized that perhaps I wasn't destined to be the low achiever everyone had expected, after all. I thought that if I could master a deck of cards, what else was I capable of accomplishing? Slowly, with every new indication that I could build myself an amazing memory, I began to gain self-confidence and self-belief and a world of opportunities opened up before me.

Now, my rather flaccid memory muscle of yesteryear has been seriously put through its paces. A strict regime of memory training over the course of 25 years has turned it into something that is beautifully toned and of which I am immensely proud. What a pity that I didn't discover and practise the art of memory when I was at school!

In this book I want to show you how you can train your memory not only to make it perform mental acrobatics the like of which you've never thought yourself capable of, but also to give you a massive boost in confidence, just as I have had. When you get a glimpse of what potential lies within your memory, you'll soon realize that that potential is applicable to other aspects of your brain power, too – from your powers of concentration and your ability to think on your feet (your "fluid intelligence") to your confidence as a narrator or speaker and even your ability to be thrown into a gathering of people you don't know and work the room like it's exactly where you belong.

By taking you along the path of my own journey of discovery, mapping the routes and byways that brought me to where I am – and who I am – today, I hope I can give you the tools to find your own amazing memory. And I hope you enjoy the ride just as much as I have.

Dominic O'Brien

HOW TO USE THIS BOOK

Unlike so many other guides to memory improvement, this book is not intended as an exhaustive introduction to every memory technique out there. Instead, it is an unveiling of my own journey into the power of memory and of my own discoveries about how the human brain works. I have won the World Memory Championships eight times so far and I've been able to do that because, by trial and error, and by careful, faithful perseverance and dedication, I've uncovered the specific techniques that have given me a perfect (well, near-perfect!) memory. This book is my way to share those techniques with you in ways that I know work – because these were the ways that worked for me.

In order to get the most out of the book, try to resist dipping in and out of it, reading the chapters by random selection. In the first half of the book, each chapter builds on the discoveries that come before – so, some techniques or details may not make sense if you haven't read the information in sequence. The second half of the book provides all the various ways you can apply the techniques, either for dedicated practice or in day-to-day life, as well as some tips on how to make sure that your body is healthy as well as your mind – another important aspect of memory training.

You might wonder how long it's going to take for the techniques to work. There are no fixed guidelines on this. Some techniques may click with you instantly, some may take more practice. The important thing is that you don't give up. I do suggest, though, that you don't move on to a new technique or new challenge in your memory training until you're completely confident with the step before. It's pointless, for example, trying to memorize a full deck of cards if you haven't yet made it past 20 cards without error. If you try to do too much too soon, you'll only become frustrated and you're more likely to give up altogether.

The other important thing is that, while the book provides you with the methods, you'll need to do the practice. If you like, you can dedicate time each day to memorizing some cards or a sequence of numbers, but actually daily life presents all sorts of opportunities for notching up practice time without feeling that you have to make a special effort. I cover this in Chapter 27.

There are 15 exercises in the book, too. The first and last are benchmark tests – you'll be able to see how far you've come by the improvement in your scores. The other 13 relate to specific aspects of memory training and they encourage you to practise skills or repeat certain challenges that develop memory power. Several of them include timed elements. It's really important that when you're memorizing you don't clock-watch, so I strongly urge that you attempt these exercises using a timer with an alarm that you can set to go off when the allocated time is up.

Most of all, though, try to keep an open mind. Read the techniques and try the exercises with a positive attitude, because I'm certain that succeeding starts with believing. Good luck!

CHAPTER ONE

YOUR MEMORY, MY MEMORY

The human brain has two halves, or hemispheres: the left and the right. It is now commonly accepted and understood that the left hemisphere governs activity in the right side of the body and the right hemisphere governs activity in the left side of the body. This may explain why tests show that I am right-brain dominant: I'm a left-hander at most activities. I write and throw with my left hand and I kick a ball with my left foot (and I was my school soccer team's left winger). But exactly how do the hemispheres of the brain work and is it as simple as all that?

Theories on left–right hemispheric functions of the brain are constantly changing. In 1981, the Nobel committee awarded its coveted medicine prize to neuropsychologist Roger Sperry for his work on split-brain research. Sperry showed that each hemisphere in the brain is responsible for specific functions. So which side does what? Since the 1980s the convention has been to say that the left hemisphere is responsible for sequence, logic, speech, analysis and numeracy; while the right is involved with imagination, colour, rhythm, dimension and spatial awareness. However, more recent research suggests that the distinction cannot be that clear-cut.

Now psychologists believe that both hemispheres have a hand in all in these functions – it's just that the two sides process the functions in different ways. For example, we now believe that the left hemisphere is more concerned with details, whereas the right hemisphere looks at the bigger picture. The way in which we store and understand language makes a really good example. Although the left brain may be responsible for storing and sequencing words, the right brain is concerned with such things as intonation and humour – that is, how someone's tone of voice can influence how we interpret the words that are spoken.

Take the phrase "Get out of here!" If someone said this to you with a happy, friendly lilt in their voice, it would be an expression of surprise or incredulity. If you got up to leave – to literally "get out of here" – you would be displaying a dip in right-brain function. You have taken the words literally – which is a left-brain characteristic. The suggestion is that the left side of the brain has little or no sense of humour, while the right side takes a wider, less literal view of the world and decides what sort of detail the left side should concentrate on.

Getting your memory into shape, I believe, is about getting the two sides of your brain to collaborate in the most effective ways possible. I'm going to teach you to apply logic, order and thought (left-brain tendencies) to imaginative, colourful and humorous images (right-brain tendencies) to get everything working in perfect synchrony. Best of all, you won't feel like you're having to try that hard – with a bit of practice, harmonizing the two sides of your brain will start to come naturally, and your memory will start to feel like it's getting bigger, better and stronger every day.

INSIDE MY MIND: RIGHT-BRAINER

I can remember that when I was at school, I spent a lot of classroom time staring out of the window, wishing I was somewhere else, or staring aimlessly at the teacher's face, but not actually concentrating on the words he or she was speaking. Most of the time I was daydreaming. You might think that my daydreams were fantastical stories with some underlying logic, but they weren't – they were haphazard, unfocused. I would allow my mind to shoot off at tangents and switch storylines quickly and at random. I wonder whether my left brain simply wasn't in a fit enough state to process details for any reasonable period of time, which meant that my right brain was constantly left unchecked, allowed to roam free. Although at the time this meant disaster for my schooldays, I believe that my ability to see things from all angles has left me open to the creativity that's so essential in memory training.

You try first: Check out your memory

In order to give yourself a benchmark by which you can measure your improvement as you learn the techniques in this book, you'll need a starting point. On the following pages I've provided two baseline tests that I give to all my students to get a measure of their existing memory power.

Short-term memory can comfortably hold chunks of around only seven to nine pieces of information – that's why, excluding the dialling code, telephone numbers tend to be six or seven digits long. In addition, rote learning, or learning by repetition, is not necessarily the best way to commit something to memory. So using a strategy will produce the best test results.

Have a go at each of the tests. If you find them tricky, it's almost certainly because I haven't taught you the best strategies for memorizing yet. If you feel that you score poorly on either or both tests – don't be too hard on yourself! Keep a note of your scores and then, once you've read the book and are confident about using the techniques, try the comparison tests at the end of the book – I hope that my experiences of working with memory, and the discoveries I've made and techniques that I've taught myself along the way, will enable you to stretch your memory closer to its true potential. Mind you, I have to say that, so far, I have found the potential of my own memory – and all the memories I've helped to train – to be infinite!

EXERCISE 1: Scoring Your Baseline Memory

These two tests will give you a baseline memory reading against which you can measure your progress as you learn the techniques in this book. The first test contains a list of 30 words that you must memorize in the exact order. The second test contains a list of numbers that you must also memorize in the correct order. Your time limit is 3 minutes for each test – set a timer so that you don't have to keep looking up to see how much time you have left. The scoring systems are given at the end of each test.

TEST 1: Three-minute words

Try memorizing the following words in the correct order (beginning with the first column on the left and reading down) with the correct spellings. You have 3 minutes to perform the memorization and as long as you need to write the words down once the time is up. No peeking!

VIOLIN	ORCHESTRA	PENCIL
KNIGHT	HERRING	STAMP
SUITCASE	FILE	RAINBOW
NECKLACE	WINDOW	CARPET
SNOWBALL	TABLE	PEACH
BABY	WRINKLE	CORK
MASK	BALL	PLANET
ROSE	PHOTO	MAGAZINE
STEEPLE	ELEPHANT	GOLD
GINGER	TROPHY	WATCH

Scoring: Score one mark per word if the word is in the right position in the sequence. Deduct one mark for a positional error (say, if you missed a word, or got a word in the wrong place). If you transpose two words, you deduct two points, but then if the next word is correct, scoring resumes as if you'd never made a mistake. The average score for students between the ages of ten and 14 for the word test is 9.5, but I would expect adults to score slightly higher.

TEST 2: Three-minute numbers

Try memorizing the following numbers in the correct order, reading left to right. You have 3 minutes to perform the memorization and then as long as you need to write the numbers down from memory once the 3 minutes are up. As before – no peeking!

1	7	1	8	9	4	6	4	3	9
2	5	3	7	3	2	4	8	5	6
4	6	9	3	7	8	3	1	7	8

Scoring: Write down as many numbers as you can recall and in the correct sequence. Score one point for a correct number, and deduct one point for any number that is wrong or out of place (if you get two numbers round the wrong way, you deduct two points; but scoring resumes if the following number is correct, as with the words test). School students averagely score 12 for this test, but, again as with the word test, I would expect an adult's score to be slightly higher.

CHAPTER TWO

HOW IT ALL BEGAN

Memory is a function of the brain that most of us take for granted. Forgetful people, the kind who frequently miss friends' or relatives' birthdays, fail to recall names or have to make a second trip to the local store because they forgot to buy something, may exclaim to themselves, "I wish I had a better memory!," but it's unlikely that they invest these words with true, deeply felt meaning. Few of us bother to stop and appreciate what an incredible, vital tool memory really is. Let's do a little thought experiment. Just imagine for a few moments what your life would be like without your wonderful memory. You would have no mental picture of friends, of family or of once-familiar surroundings. In effect you would lose your identity. Your sense of where you belong (with particular people and places) would be gone. Self-image partly revolves around mistakes you have learned from and achievements you are proud of, and these too would be obliterated. To have no sense of belonging, of your full, complicated self with all its bumps and angles, would be tragic.

Conversely, a fully functioning, powerful memory is not only a practical instrument, equipping us to do everyday things such as call a relative, or find our keys, or bake a pizza: it also provides us with a huge source of personal, inner wealth. I have learned that my memory is far greater than all the things I've stored in it – it gives me self-confidence, reassurance, and an inherent strength of belief in who I am. But more of that later. First, I want to take you right back to the start of my memory journey, which began in 1987 when I was 30 years old. I watched a memory man, Creighton Carvello, recall a random sequence of 52 cards on TV, and I was fascinated to know how he could achieve such an impressive, apparently almost superhuman feat of memory power. Was he a genius or did he use a strategy? Was he a freak of nature or just really clever?

Armed with a deck of cards I set about trying to replicate his achievement. However, like most people, I could manage to recall only the first five or six cards before being overwhelmed by the confusing sequence of numbers and suits. I wondered how on Earth Carvello had been able to achieve this apparent miracle of the mind. Such is my nature that the mystery became all-consuming. I felt compelled to investigate the curiosity of Creighton Carvello's mind from all angles. Why? Because I believed that if he could do it, I could, too.

My starting point was a game I remembered playing as a child to help while away the hours on endless car journeys – we called it "I packed in my bag". You've probably played it yourself – in turn, each player adds an item to the list of what's in the bag, repeating everything that's gone before: "I packed in my bag a book," then "I packed in my bag a book and an umbrella" and so on. When a player forgets an item, he or she is out, until there's one winner. Although I was quite good at the game, like the vast majority of people I simply repeated the words over and over again in my head in the hope that they would somehow stick, sometimes picturing the items laid out in a row to help me along. Overall, though, I don't remember using any particular strategy to make the game any easier or my ability at it any better.

I thought about this game in light of what I'd seen of Creighton Carvello's challenge, but it soon became obvious that he wasn't using repetition to make the sequence of cards stick – he turned each card over and looked at it just once before turning the next. He didn't ever go back and review the cards or, indeed, look at any of them again, so he wasn't obviously going over the sequence to embed it. In which case, what *was* he doing? And, more to the point, how exactly was I going to memorize 52 playing cards with just one deal?

I pondered whether I could code parts of my body to move in a certain way depending on what cards I turned up. For example, if the first card was the 3 Clubs, I might turn my head by what felt like three degrees; if the second card was the King of Spades, I might move my tongue into my left cheek and so on. There wasn't any immediate connection between the movements and the cards I attributed to them, but I hoped that if somehow I learned the physical codes and used them in my memorization attempts, the sequence would stick more readily than just the names of the cards. Pretty quickly I realized that this system was impracticable, so as an alternative I considered whether a mathematical formula might be helpful. For example, if the first two cards were 4 and 8, I could multiply the two to get 32 – but then how would I memorize 32? And how was I going to incorporate the suit? None of my systems seemed to quite work.

It didn't take long before I realized that parts of the body and mathematics were red herrings. I remember going to my local library to see if the solution could be found in a book, but at that time there were no books on memory training, and I couldn't look it up on the Internet, because the Internet as we know it hadn't been invented. The only way I was going to find the answer, if at all, was by trial and error.

While logic and powers of deduction had to play a part (although I wasn't quite sure what part yet), it soon dawned on me that the key to success lay within my imagination and creativity. I had heard that creating a story was a way to memorize information, so I toyed with this idea. The minutes ran into hours and then days. I began to "recognize" people and objects in the cards (see p.43), so that eventually I was able to memorize a dozen or so cards without error. I used my budding card codes to create a story for each sequence, and this seemed to work. To my mind this was small but significant progress and it certainly provided me with enough incentive to persist with the idea until I could do exactly what Creighton Carvello had done.

It was only really a matter of days since my first flirtation with this memory challenge before I succeeded. Using a combination of the story method and the use of locus, or place (but more about that later), I recalled the sequence of 52 cards without error. To this day, when I bring back the memory of that moment, I recapture in perfect detail what it felt like finally to have done it. This wasn't just an achievement, it was utterly empowering. I'd never felt like this before, I was drunk on it and I certainly wasn't going to stop there. Within a relatively short space of time, through curiosity,

INSIDE MY MIND: SETTING MY IMAGINATION FREE

Once I had begun to try to find the key to equalling the feat of Creighton Carvello, and I started to really explore the weird and wonderful things my brain had to offer, I noticed that I was becoming more creative. The harder I worked my memory, the more ideas and associations would fire seemingly from all directions. At the heart of my system (which I'll teach you over the following chapters) lay the process of transforming playing cards into mental pictures. To begin with, this process was slow and sluggish, but after a while a steady, effortless stream of colourful thoughts and pictures would pop into my mind automatically. Soon I was applying the same methods to memorize gigantic sequences of numbers; long lists of words; hundreds of binary numbers and combinations of names and faces; and telephone numbers, facts and figures, poetry and much more. Becoming a memory man, I believe, unlocked my creativity – a creativity that had been inhibited by years of being told to calm down and concentrate at school. Suddenly, my mind was free!

persistence, trial and error and sheer determination, I'd used my strategy to memorize, not one, but several decks of cards after just a single sighting of each card. In the process I'd begun a journey that was to transform my powers of recall – and much more besides. I believe that those first few steps set in motion a sequence of events that would result in a complete overhaul of the multiple functions of my brain, beginning with my creativity.

CHAPTER THREE

MEMORY AND CREATIVITY

It may sound dramatic to say that my experiences with memory have overhauled my brain, but memory is so bound up with creativity – and the many aspects of brain function that involve creativity – that you'll soon see this isn't such an over-the-top statement at all. Most importantly, training your memory draws heavily upon the resources of your imagination. Even during my earliest adventures into the powers of my memory, while I was still trying to emulate the great Creighton Carvello, I realized that to memorize a string of unconnected data, such as sequences of cards, involves first coding them into images. In this way, the pieces of unconnected information can somehow become connected together. I now know that this process of using imagination brings into play a whole range of brain functions, including logic and spatial awareness.

Some people are concerned that they don't have a strong enough imagination to make memory training possible for them. If you're one such person, banish that thought! Don't you sometimes sit at your desk at work imagining yourself in great detail somewhere more exotic or – if you're having a stressful day – calming? If you let time slip, you may even find that you've created a whole imaginary world with precision accuracy. I believe that we all possess incredible powers of imagination – it's just that often we've been taught or conditioned to suppress them. I want to reassure you that it's never too late to unleash your imagination.

I certainly know about this – remember how as a child I was often criticized for being a daydreamer? My teachers did all they could to suppress the imaginative me. Now, however, I've learned to appreciate that my early tendency to daydream merely showed my powers of creative thinking. Yes, my daydreams were bizarre and skittish, but I think they were my mind's way to express its infinite, random potential for creativity – a potential that I'm sure is the reason I've been able to excel in memory competitions. That potential is there in all of us, if we can learn (or re-learn, as I had to) to let it out.

Imaginative thinking is definitely something that comes naturally to me – today, more quickly and effortlessly than ever. However, if you feel that it's not natural for you, I'm certain that the practical exercises and all the advice and tips you'll encounter throughout this book will teach you how to tap in to your imagination in a variety of ways. The more you exercise your imagination in the ways I suggest, the easier it will become to think creatively – to generate images, ideas and thoughts – in all walks of your life. Furthermore, as your imagination becomes livelier, so will your brain power, including your memory, become stronger. You'll find that you're able to think faster and with greater clarity whether you're deciding what to wear, how to memorize a deck of cards or how to pitch for a sales deal. All that's required from you is to allow that dream-maker to come out to play.

INSIDE MY MIND: THE MAKING OF A DAYDREAMER?

The following is a true account of an incident that took place at a railway station on April 24, 1958. A young mother and her children had been visiting an aunt on the south coast of England and were returning home by train from St Leonards-on-Sea. As they were waiting at the platform, the mother decided to buy a magazine to read on the journey home and left her young son to hold on to the pushchair and in it his contented eight-month-old baby brother. As the mother walked into the newsagents, a train departed from the platform and headed toward a tunnel. At this point the young boy decided he, too, wanted something to read on the train and let go of the pushchair to follow his mother.

As the train headed out of the station, causing a backdraft, the pushchair started to move, found the platform slope and picked up speed. On its descent it collided with the very last section of the train, which then pulled the pushchair along with it. At this point, the mother, hearing the commotion, rushed outside and, screaming in horror, watched her baby being carried off to what she thought was certain death.

I was that baby. Miraculously, I am alive to tell the story – a bump on my forehead was the only outward sign of what had happened. However, I believe that that bump was to map out the rest of my life, because I think this single event could have accounted for the attention problems I had as a child. If it did, in a peculiar way I'm somewhat grateful to it, because without my tendencies toward daydreaming perhaps I'd never have discovered my own perfect memory.

EXERCISE 2: Imagining the Senses

This exercise is designed to loosen up your imagination so that you get used to the idea of making unconventional associations – not just by using visual images, but by engaging all your senses (this will prove essential for creating memorizations that will stick). Practise it daily if you can, until you're really confident that you can make vivid, imaginative links between things that at first seem unconnected. Once you've read the instructions, close your eyes if this makes it easier to flesh out the images and sensations.

SCENARIO 1
Imagine you're holding a football in your hands. Imagine that it smells of freshly squeezed oranges. Take a few moments to bring those two thoughts to life in your mind. Now imagine the football has the texture of jelly. It's ticking like a clock and tastes of chocolate. Don't rush – dwell on the image for at least 5 minutes, making it as vivid as you can. If your mind wanders, bring it back to the first sensation of holding the football.

SCENARIO 2
Once you've fully engaged with the first scenario, try this one: Imagine a yellow elephant with pink spots. It mews like a cat, tastes of ginger and has the texture of stinging nettles and the aroma of fresh coffee beans. Again, spend at least 5 minutes making all this come alive in your mind.

When you're ready, test yourself by recalling the strange qualities of that football and of the elephant. The more detailed you made the visualizations, the easier you'll find it to bring the images back to mind.

CHAPTER FOUR

THE POWER OF ASSOCIATION

I hope that the exercise at the end of the last chapter has shown you how capable you are of conjuring up associations between themes or notions that at first may seem completely disconnected, by engaging your senses. This is your first step to a perfect memory. However, to make that step really worthwhile, you need to be able to make the links as strong as possible and at speed. Happily, your brain is a powerful machine when it comes to association – it wants to make links, and it wants to make them fast. The problems lie not with your brain itself, but with the "interference" that prevents you from thinking freely – that upsets your mental footfalls, causing you to stumble every now and then.

If you find that interference is hampering your ability to think freely and creatively, you have to do what I did and learn to let go. Don't try to slow down your brain or clear the inner noise, and don't try to make sense of how the associations are connected together; just trust that they are connected and let the pure power of association "happen".

I believe that we are, in a sense, preconditioned to pigeonhole our experiences into certain categories. If I said to you the word "strawberry", I suspect that a picture of a strawberry would come into your mind. There it is – fat and red with a green stalk. But if you let your mind go, set it free, what happens? The simple image of the strawberry will still ping up, but perhaps you can taste it this time? Or maybe you can smell it? Is the skin pitted or glistening? Is the strawberry growing on a plant, or is it in a bowl with other strawberries? If you let your mind wander freely, the chances are that the associations will get both broader and richer. They'll become more vivid. Perhaps you remember a day when you went on a picnic and ate strawberries. Were you with a friend? Were the strawberries dipped in chocolate or dunked in cream? What was the friend wearing and what did you talk about? And there you go, your mind is off again – the reminiscence you have sets off another string of associations until you end up far from where you started; your last imaginings before you come back to the real world might have nothing obviously to do with strawberries at all.

In the same way, the French novelist Marcel Proust wrote an autobiographical novel called *Remembrance of Things Past*, which he spun from the stream of memories that were triggered by the taste of Madeleine cake dipped in linden tea.

The point here is that, allowed free rein, your memory will take you to untold places. Every time you set your imagination free, you set your memory free to make associations with lightning speed and great accuracy and strength. Speed, accuracy and strength in associations are all essential components of having a perfect memory.

CHAPTER FIVE

DIMENSIONS OF ASSOCIATION

Other than how fast – even instantaneous – associations can be, what your free association on a strawberry and Proust's novel teach us, in particular, is that making associations is not a simple, one-dimensional thing. First, your emotions come into play. Probably before you remember the details of any episode from your past, you remember how you felt about it. For example, do you remember the day you learned to ride a bicycle? When I think about this, the first thing that comes back to me is the feeling of elation – and slight panic – when I realized I was responsible for staying upright all by myself. Once your emotions have brought the event alive again, then come the senses. Smell has strong links with memory: the olfactory bulb (the hub of the sense of smell) and parts of the brain associated with memory and learning have a close physiological connection. So you might first remember the scents that were around you as you pedalled off. Or perhaps it's sound that comes back first – you might remember the wind whooshing through your ears. Alternatively, think how a piece of music can make a memory more vivid (often it triggers more emotional feedback). Or perhaps it's the sights around you that come flooding back – you may have a sharp image of how the scene around you looked, especially if there was something particularly bright, vivid or unusual in it.

When I train students to allow their minds to associate freely, I ask them to think about not the first time they rode a bike, but their first day at school. Try it now. You might have a vague recollection of the walk up to the building and maybe a mental glimpse of the teacher who welcomed you, but I bet the first vivid thing you remember is how you felt. I remember feeling excited but apprehensive. I *sort of* wanted to go, but overwhelmingly I didn't want to leave the security of home. I also remember that once I was there, on that first day at least, I was happy. I remember laughing a lot with my new friends. Then come my sensual memories. I remember the smell of the tarmac in the playground (a smell that still reminds me of that first day), the sound of the bell that called us in for our first lessons, and even the taste of school milk – it seemed thicker and more creamy than milk from home. I remember the ice-cold feel of the milk bottle and the exact blue of the thin straw that we used to pierce the shiny milk-bottle top and drink through.

If you can hone your natural ability to make connections and bring alive episodes from your past by using your emotions and senses, as well as logic and creativity, you make it easier for your brain to memorize new information in an instantly vivid, memorable way. In addition, you get used to the sense of letting your brain make the fastest connections and trusting them. Instant association is an important aspect of memory training, because first associations will prove to be the most reliable. I shall come back to this point again and again over the course of this book.

EXERCISE 3: Memory "Free Play"

Words evoke memories. Look at each of the following words to see what flashes from the past they bring up for you. You need only glance at each word for a second or two. Try not to edit what you remember, just allow your first associations to happen. Then, let the images, thoughts, emotions and senses resurface in as much detail as possible – it may take moments, or it may take several minutes – and then move on to the next word. The aim of this exercise is merely to get you used to free-associating and letting not only images but also emotions and sensations flood back. Although this doesn't feel like it's going to make a memory champion of you, trust me – the better and more practised you are at this kind of free association, the more accomplished you'll become at memorizing.

KITTEN

RAINBOW

TOY

BIRTHDAY

ICE CREAM

SNOW

CHURCH

CUSHION

SAND

TOE NAIL

The exercise on the previous page will help you to get into the habit of recapturing not only events, but the thoughts, sensations and emotions that go with them. You also need to feel comfortable with the speed with which a memory or memories can come alive.

When I do this exercise – and other exercises like it – I travel back and forth through my life. I find myself in different locations, with different people, feeling different emotions and hearing, seeing, smelling, touching and tasting different things. The reminiscences come so thick and fast it's like being on a rollercoaster, zipping this way and that way through my personal history. I hope it felt at least a bit like this for you, too.

INSIDE MY MIND: MY EARLIEST MEMORY

Words evoke memories, and whenever I hear the word "cot", I find myself transported to my earliest memory of all. I must have been aged about two and I was shaking the bars of my cot, enjoying the feeling of bouncing up and down with an endless stream of energy. I can even remember my mother telling me she thought I was limbering up my muscles, like a boxer on the edge of the boxing ring. It constantly amazes me how much, how far back, can be triggered in the brain if it is left unhindered, to roam free into its deepest recesses.

CHAPTER SIX

CHAINS OF ASSOCIATION

Now that you know how your brain can supply you with a flood of memories triggered instantly by just a single word, you need to take the next step and look at forging links between two words that have no apparent connection. We've talked about imagination and we've talked about using your past to make associations – when you put the two together, I think you have the key to the most basic skill in the art of memorization.

Without points of reference in your past, I believe it would be impossible to make connections between any two concepts (whether they are words, objects, activities or whatever). Your past provides you with learning and you need to use that learning to create pathways from one thing to another. Everything in your life fits together like pieces of a jigsaw. To get from one piece of the jigsaw to another, you can link them piece by piece. The most efficient way to create that pathway is to use the fewest pieces of the jigsaw possible – to find the most obvious connections from your bank of knowledge.

Let's say I want to memorize two words: wall and chicken. I have an endless stream of memories associated with both these words and I just have to find the pathway that links one to the other in my mind. For example:

Wall makes me think of the Pink Floyd album, a wall I climbed as a child, the wall I used to jump over on my way out of school and so on. As the associations come thick and fast, I come across the most obvious link: the traditional nursery rhyme "Humpty Dumpty sat on a wall." Eureka! Humpty Dumpty sits on a **wall** and he is an egg – eggs are laid by **chickens**. I use my imagination to visualize a chicken laying Humpty the egg on a wall. I make the associations vivid by recalling my childhood self singing the nursery rhyme and, automatically, I imagine "little me" giggling at the image of the chicken laying Humpty. This may not have happened in my actual past, but the link between little me and the rhyme is enough to create a logical scenario for my reaction. This all sounds laborious and long-winded – but in practice my brain makes the connections in little more than an instant.

Here's another example: pen and soup. In what ways can you connect them so that you remember them both? Using free association and my imagination, I come up with the following possibilities: use the pen to stir the soup (perhaps the soup changes colour as the ink from the pen mixes in); use the pen to make a pattern or perhaps write a word in the thick soup; fill the pen with soup as though it were ink to write a letter; use the pen as a straw for the soup; and so on. Although the connections to my past aren't obvious in this example, all the associations draw upon my experience and understanding of both a pen and a bowl of soup. Memory and association are inseparable.

Practise the same principles for yourself using the exercise opposite. If this is your first attempt at this sort of exercise, you may well find yourself deliberating over some of the pairs

EXERCISE 4: Forging Links

Look at these pairs of words and, like someone netting a butterfly, catch hold of the first association that comes into your head to link them together. Don't be tempted to edit the links – just set your brain free to find the most obvious pathway from one word to the other in the pair. Once you've finished, cover the right-hand column and see how many of the pairings you can recall. If you can recall ten or more pairings, you can be confident that your associations are starting to stick. Keep practising until you can recall all 14 words.

BUS	SALT
TABLE	MOON
GUITAR	PLASTER
ANKLE	GLASS
CORK	TORCH
BEETHOVEN	MOBILE PHONE
MARBLE	CANDLE
GOOSE	BUBBLE
ELASTIC	SHARK
ORANGE	RIFLE
PEN	ROOF
DAISY	MOUSE
CAMERA	SHOE
BRACELET	HAIRBRUSH

of words. The goal is to allow your brain to arrive at whatever common denominator it wants to find without prejudice or preconceptions getting in the way. Mobile phones hadn't been invented in Beethoven's day, but you still might imagine the composer using one to call his agent; or, if your brain prefers audio cues, perhaps you imagine your phone going off with a Beethoven's Fifth Symphony ringtone. All you have to do is to allow the fastest common denominator to enter your head. Don't try to make the connection any more weird or fantastical than it needs to be – there's no need to make your creativity work overtime. The more natural and logical the imagined scenario is to you, the more likely it is that the two halves of your brain are working in harmony and your brain will accept and remember the associations you come up with.

Once you've completed the exercise, congratulate yourself. You've just mastered the basic technique for memorizing unconnected information. It's called the Link Method. Now that you've used it for pairs of words, you can use it to memorize lists.

CHAPTER SEVEN

THE LINK METHOD

Let's take the first five words from the test I asked you to do right at the beginning of the book. The first five words are Violin, Knight, Suitcase, Necklace, Snowball. If we run with the principle that everything can be connected to everything else, all that you need to do to memorize this list is to create a link between each of the items on it. Imagine you hear the sweet sound of a violin, which is being played by a knight. In your mind's eye see how tricky it is for him to position the violin under his chin with all that armour in the way. By his feet there's a suitcase, perhaps it's a vivid colour, or perhaps it's rather battered and old. You open the suitcase and find a priceless diamond necklace – sunlight bounces off the diamonds making them sparkle brightly; the reflected glare makes you squint. As you turn your head away, a snowball hits you on the cheek – you feel the icy sting as it makes impact. Remember that the more you practise using all your senses and emotional responses to make your associations, the more adept your brain will become at crafting them quickly and the more memorable the connections will be.

Replay this short scene in your mind – add some more detail if you need to. Once you've done that efficiently (my links might not be the most resonant for you, of course), you should have no problem repeating the list of items forwards – and even backwards – simply by replaying the story. If you can repeat the order of items in both directions, you prove that the list is well and truly cemented in your memory. Now, can you instantly recall the two words either side of the suitcase without running through the complete list of five? If you can, your brain has fully assimilated and integrated the new data so that you're now able to reproduce it (recall it) in a variety of ways. Being able to remember, interpret, reinterpret and if necessary reconstruct is at the heart of how we assess everything we learn.

When I teach the Link Method, I ask my students how long they think they will remember the list of five words. Most say that it will take only a few minutes before they've forgotten them again – but they are soon surprised to find that's far from the truth. The method is so powerful that often the list sticks for well over 24 hours. I doubt anyone would have that level of success merely by repeating the words over and over to learn by rote.

Admittedly, though, this is a mere five words, so let's add two items and apply the link method to the following seven objects: Boat, Tyre, Parcel, Button, Cabbage, Mouse, Boot.

The story I come up with is that I'm drifting lazily in a **boat** on a calm sea. As I approach the shore, I see a **tyre** lying in the sand. I roll the tyre along the sand and it lands by a **parcel**. As I unwrap the parcel to see what's inside, I find a gadget with a bright red push **button**. Curiosity gets the better of me and as I press the button, magically a **cabbage** materializes from beneath the sand. Out of the cabbage appears a frightened **mouse**, which scuttles away to hide in a **boot** that's been discarded further up the beach.

What I find most fascinating is that while learning by rote and repetition can take hours, and often still produces poor results, learning using the Link Method is quick (how long did the story take to conjure up? 30 or 40 seconds?), and the recall is usually impeccable. It's all about context. The Link Method attaches significance to unconnected pieces of information. We put them in a context that attaches them to the real world, with some form of logic, and they become memorable.

A trick of the mind

I think using the first person is important here, too. By putting yourself in the story (you don't imagine *me* floating in the boat, you see yourself), you somehow trick your brain into believing that the experience has actually happened to you.

However, you can trick your brain like this only if you've made the images as true to life as possible, and that means using all your senses. What can you see as you drift lazily on the boat? What can you hear as you approach the shore? Can you smell the tyre's rubber as it gets hot in the sun? What colour is the wrapping on the parcel? How does the sand feel against your feet as you run along the beach to chase the tyre? The more vivid you make your associations, the more readily they'll come back to you.

Another reason that the first person works so well is that, if you are part of the story, you will have feelings and emotions attached to what happens. You probably felt relaxed and contented floating along on the water. Perhaps you were slightly panicky or anxious as the tyre ran away from you. You were probably a little bit apprehensive when you pushed the red button. Once you bring your humanity, vulnerability and "realness" to your story, your brain can believe it as true – and that makes it even more memorable. Interestingly, the circuitry of your brain – that is, the individual neurons and networks of neurons it contains – can't tell the difference between what's real and what you've imagined. Only "you" as a whole conscious being know the truth – that's why tricking your brain is really relatively easy.

Powers of visualization

Over the years, I've had many people come to me to say they're afraid that these sorts of techniques will be lost on them because they simply don't believe they have the creativity they need to make the images stick. However, it's really important to remember that the things you imagine should be within the realms of possibility; or at least hold some form of logic – so while they're creative, they aren't too fantastical. They might be a bit bizarre or unconventional, but in theory perfectly plausible or possible. Think back to the pen and soup scenario in Chapter 6. I admit it's unlikely that anyone would ever use a pen to stir a bowl of soup; or that you might use the soup as ink for the pen. But it's not *completely* impossible. Similarly, do you remember Beethoven on a mobile phone? Alright, Beethoven would not have had a mobile, but if he had had one, he'd probably have used it to call his agent. There is always some logic to the scenario, and yes, you need to be creative, but not superhumanly so.

I also want to reassure you by making a confession: now that memorizing by association is second nature to me, my mental images aren't at all refined in every detail. Sometimes they are sketches with only the right colour and shapes; sometimes they are cartoon-like. I certainly don't produce perfect visual representations. I conjure up ideas and scenarios – images that are just enough to make the connection in my head. However, for now, if you're just starting out, I recommend that you fill in your images as much as possible: only once you're really comfortable and confident in the practice should you start short-cutting.

Becoming a storyteller

There's another aspect of the Link Method that I haven't really touched upon, and that's order. In the baseline test that I set you at the beginning of the book, I asked you to memorize not just the words, but also the order in which they appeared. In fact, if you remember, you were penalized for not getting the order exactly right. To avoid penalty points, you have to make links from one object to the next in the "correct" order. The easiest way to do this is to create a story that incorporates all the items in the list one after the other. The story, like all good stories, takes on a logic of its own, which reinforces the order of the items, because the sequence of their appearance is meaningful to the whole context. When you replay the story, following it logically from one scenario to the next, you should recall all the items in the right order, too. Try the exercise on the following page to get a better sense of how this works. If you forget any of the words in the list during the recall, the links you made in the story weren't strong enough – have another go.

EXERCISE 5: Memory Storytelling

In this exercise, use the Link Method to create a story that enables you to memorize the following ten words in order. Your own story will always be more effective than one I create for you, so I don't want to give you any pointers except to say there is no time limit to this exercise. You can take as long as you need to get the story right – but remember that the first, ideally instantaneous connections you make will probably be the strongest anyway. Allow your mind to think intuitively and use all your senses. Once you've created your story, cover the page and write down the words in the correct order. If you didn't score ten out of ten, your story's links weren't strong enough – go back and strengthen any weak links in the chain.

BICYCLE

COMPUTER

LADDER

PILLOW

CAMERA

BOOMERANG

CAKE

DIARY

SOAP

GIRAFFE

CHAPTER EIGHT

EUREKA! MY FIRST SUCCESSFUL ATTEMPT

Now that I've explained to you how important it is to use association, I can tell you how it was that I finally cracked what Creighton Carvello was doing. I realized I needed to stop making lists and stop searching outside myself for the answers, and instead tap into some of that wonderful creativity that was bubbling away inside me already. You have that same creativity inside you, too, which is why I know that my techniques can transform your memory just as they did mine.

So, how did I memorize my first deck of cards? I started by staring at individual cards to see if they reminded me of something familiar – an object or person from my life. For example, I looked at the Jack of Hearts and the face reminded me of my uncle. The 5 Spades looked to me like a hand held out with four fingers and thumb. The 10 Diamonds reminded me of the door to 10 Downing Street (Diamonds reminded me of money or wealth and 10 Downing Street is where the Prime Minister looks after the UK's prosperity; also the address cued the abbreviation for the card: "10 D"). To memorize these three cards in sequence, I linked the people and objects together – in exactly the same way that you learned to link the unconnected words in the last exercise. I imagined my uncle (Jack of Hearts) using his fist (5 Spades) to knock on the door of Number 10 (10 Diamonds).

Over the course of many hours, I slowly but surely gave every card in the deck a new identity, until finally I had coded each with its own unique association. I shuffled the deck and set to work.

The first full deck took just under half an hour to link together into a story. I had my uncle flying through clouds and firing oranges from a hammock that was dripping with honey. Jack Nicklaus (a golfer, so my King of Clubs) was hoovering up a pair of ducks (2 Hearts, because 2 is represented by ducks in the number–shape system – see pp.82–4 – and the Hearts reminded me of little upturned beaks), which were spitting at a snowman (8 Diamonds – the snowman is the number–shape for 8 and I imagined icicles hanging round his neck like diamonds). At the end of this rather exhausting Alice-in-Wonderland epic, I held the deck face down and prepared to recall each card in turn, revealing its true identity as I did so. I managed 41 of the 52 cards in sequence. Not bad for a first attempt!

I had made a good start – but it wasn't faultless and no matter how efficiently I used my story system, the thought of emulating Carvello's memory still seemed beyond reach. He had memorized a deck in only 2 minutes 59 seconds, and for me to get up to speed, especially to complete the feat in three minutes or less, seemed impossible. I wasn't put off, though – I was sure that complete success must lie around the corner. My obvious, measurable improvements made me even more determined to refine the system until the perfect strategy for memorizing finally came to me.

My first card codes

As I continued experimenting and practising memorizing cards using my story method, I noticed that I was able to string together short sequences of cards, but then I would hit a weak link in the chain and a card would slip through. Let me explain by giving you specific examples of my card codes from those early days and some sense of how I came up with the codes:

6 Diamonds/An aeroplane (Because the number 6 is similar in shape to the jet engine beneath the wing of a plane and flying is an expensive way to travel, which fits with the idea of Diamonds being associated with wealth or money.)

4 Diamonds/Cash (I imagined this card as a collection of four £1 coins sitting neatly in a square.)

5 Clubs/My dog (My Aunt's dog was called Sally and an "S" looks like a "5". It was my Aunt's Jack Russell that inspired me to get my own dog later on in life; I chose Clubs because a club is a weapon and Jack Russells make good ratters.)

8 Hearts/A cloud (Because an "8" reminds me of bubbly, white clouds and Hearts are similarly cloud-like to me.)

4 Spades/My car (Because the four gives me four wheels and the Spades remind me of my tyres.)

3 Spades/A forest (Because Spades are tree-shaped and because three rhymes with tree.)

The logic I applied was that card codes could fall into one of three categories: people and animals; modes of transport; and places. I adopted codes for all the cards in a deck simply by writing down all the card names, deciding on the code for each card, writing it next to the card name – and then learning each pairing. This sounds laborious, and I suppose in a sense it was, but there were certain automatic associations I made (such as 7 Diamonds as James Bond 007 in the film *Diamonds are Forever* and 9 Clubs as Ni(nine)ck Faldo, the golfer) to speed up the overall process. Besides, I stayed motivated because I knew that once I'd learned the codes, they would bring me ever closer to my goal of matching (perhaps even beating!) Carvello.

I then used the Link Method, creating stories by linking together my codes for each card in the correct sequence. Understandably, perhaps, I found that some sequences were easier to memorize than others. For example, let's say the first five cards were 3 Spades, 5 Clubs, 4 Diamonds, 6 Diamonds and 8 Hearts. I would picture the forest and in it my dog would be barking at some cash. A plane would land to collect the cash and fly into the clouds. The story had some sense of sequence and logic, so I could memorize it easily. However, any slight alterations in a sequence could cause me problems.

Let's say instead the order was 6 Diamonds, 3 Spades, 5 Clubs, 8 Hearts, 4 Diamonds. This time I would imagine a plane flying into the forest where my dog is barking. However, my dog now has to fly up into the cloud where there is some cash. The link between my dog and the cloud becomes tenuous – it lacks any believable logic, and this makes it a weakness in the chain.

But trying to hold on to logic wasn't my only problem. Not only were the links in my chains of association fragile at times, I was expending heaps of mental energy working out crazy leaps

INSIDE MY MIND: THE RUSH OF SUCCESS

A moment of clarity is an amazing thing. You must have experienced it at some point in your life, too. When I realized where I'd been going wrong, and – most importantly – how to fix it, I had a stratospheric surge in self-belief, like the alchemist turning common elements into gold. It was all the incentive I needed to practise hard, working at deck after deck of cards, until my memory could do the same and more as Creighton Carvello. It's this self-belief that I think transformed me – far more than codes or decks of cards – and taught me that anything is achievable with a will and a way, something my schooldays had singularly failed to do.

and dashes from one scene to another. It was exhausting, time-consuming and not foolproof. And then – at last – I had that "Eureka!" moment: I finally understood that I was using all the right ingredients, but in the wrong permutations. I suddenly realized that instead of designating certain cards to represent certain places, if I used a predetermined location and then made every card an object, animal or person, I could place those images at consecutive stops within that location. In that way, as long as the stops followed a natural order, and the link between each card and its location was strong enough, I would surely memorize and recall the sequence perfectly. And there it was, my Holy Grail of memory systems: "The Journey Method".

CHAPTER NINE

DEVISING THE JOURNEY METHOD

I think it's fair to say that the Journey Method was to change my life – but in its earliest forms it was far from perfect. Once I'd had my moment of clarity, I tested my theory about placement by mapping out a journey that consisted of 20 distinct stops. I knew it had to be a journey that was completely familiar to me (I didn't want to have to spend time thinking about what the next stop was) and I also knew that I'd have to make the links between the card codes and the stops on the journey really strong. So, it seemed natural to make my first journey a walk through the village where I lived. Here are the first five stages:

STAGE 1	**Front gate**
STAGE 2	**Next-door neighbour's house**
STAGE 3	**Bus stop**
STAGE 4	**Shop**
STAGE 5	**Car park**

Then I set about recoding the cards that I'd originally imagined as places so that they were now objects, because otherwise I'd have to pair up two locations and I knew this would become confusing. The 3 Spades, for example, had to change from a forest to a log; the 8 Hearts, which had been a rather vague and forgettable cloud, became me (for no reason other than the fact that I had always found this a hard card to memorize – making it represent me provided an association that is particularly strong, because I can so completely imagine how I would respond to any given situation). With a fixed route and a specific object code for each card, all I had to do was picture each code (card) at its appropriate position along the journey.

Let's say the first five cards I turn up are: 6 Diamonds, 3 Spades, 5 Clubs, 8 Hearts, 4 Diamonds. This is how I memorize them using the first five stops on my memory journey:

- I imagine an aeroplane (6 Diamonds) parked at my front gate.
- Outside my next-door neighbour's house there's a log (3 Spades) leaning against the fence.
- At the bus stop my dog (5 Clubs) jumps up and down barking at the traffic going by.
- Inside the shop I see myself (8 Hearts) buying a newspaper.
- In the car park there's a bundle of cash (4 Diamonds) in a parking space.

This time my mind couldn't get confused about the order, because the journey gave me the order effortlessly. My test run of 20 cards proved a complete success – I didn't make a single error. So, I scaled up: I extended the route so that it went from my gate, through the village, around a pub, across the cricket pitch, along a path with beautiful views to a bowling green, until I had a journey of 52 stages – just right for a whole deck of cards.

After a few more practices at mentally walking my 52-stage route without trying to memorize anything along it, it was time to trial the full deck. Would my promising strategy hold up to my greatest challenge? Yes! I managed to recall all 52 cards with no errors in less than ten minutes. At this point I knew that I could conceivably make a challenge for Creighton Carvello's 2 minutes 59 seconds – it was just a matter of time.

Overcoming the drawbacks: Ghosts on location

Perfect as my method was for a single deck, I found that some of the associations I made were so strong that when I tried to repeat the feat, I got ghostly "double" images of previous sequences, and my brain became confused as to which of the images was right for that sequence. The answer was simple: I needed more than one journey. I devised six journeys altogether, using them in rotation, so that by the time I came back to one I'd used before, the memory of the cards I'd memorized on it last time had faded.

The settings for my various journeys had to be sufficiently familiar, stimulating and interesting that I would remember the stages I picked out along them without any trouble at all. I'm a keen golfer, so the natural choices for me were a couple of my favourite golf courses, as well as houses (indoor journeys work just as well, as long as the route around the location is logical, and comes easily to you) and towns or villages that I've lived in.

A process of natural selection took place as, by trial and error, I filtered out routes that didn't work. For example, if the stages along the routes were too uniform in character, I found that they weren't memorable enough. I devised one journey made up of 52 shops in a town. But it didn't work, because I had to try too hard to remember the sequence of shops and I had trouble distinguishing one shop from another in my mind's eye. Fairly quickly I came to the conclusion that variety and contrast in the stages themselves and in my interaction with them are among the keys to a successful journey. Typically, if I base a route around a town, I find myself moving in different ways in or around stops. I make sure I travel in and out of buildings, I might go over a wall or across a stream or river. I might pop into a telephone kiosk, or stop to look at a menu in a restaurant and then wander off to look at a statue, and so on. The journey is interesting and sticks in my mind effortlessly. And once I've been through it a few times, I don't have to think about recalling it – I can mentally

INSIDE MY MIND: COPING WITH TOWN PLANNING

People often ask me whether or not I regularly update my routes to account for changes in the landscape. The answer is no. Once the routes are hard-wired they provide a track that automatically guides me from stage to stage. Updating causes disruption. In fact, I even avoid returning to old routes, if I can – I don't want to know if shops change their usage, houses are pulled down or telephone boxes are removed. I prefer to remember and use the routes just as they were.

walk through on autopilot and use it to provide hooks for me to hang information on.

Beating the drawbacks: Card cut-outs

There was one other element to my system that wasn't yet foolproof – there were certain card codes that were a bit unpredictable, a few that I kept forgetting. I realized that cards represented by people rather than objects were the easiest to recall. People can interact with the stops on my journey; they have feelings and emotions that can turn an abstract scene into something calamitous, joyous, hilarious and so on. Injecting emotion into my memorizations made them instantly more memorable. So, it was time to turn all my card codes into people (and a couple of favourite animals).

Remember the 3 Spades? First, I coded it as a forest, then a log, and then in my final round of refinement it became Malcolm, the man who used to supply me with logs for my fire. The 6 Diamonds, once an aeroplane, became Tim, a friend who used to work for an airline. So, I set to work feverishly refining my codes until I arrived at a cast-list of characters that would leave a lasting impression on my memory. They aren't all people I've known – there are plenty of famous faces in there, too. The 3 Hearts, for example, is the Beverley Sisters (a singing trio from the 1950s '60s), while the King of Clubs is no longer Jack Nicklaus, but Adolf Hitler (Clubs makes me think of aggressors). Thirty years on, now that my master race of unforgettable card characters is in place, I rarely alter the codes, because I have no need. And there's one card that's very special, because it's never been altered: I'm proud to say that the 5 Clubs to this day is my dear old dog.

CHAPTER TEN

USING THE JOURNEY METHOD

To remember in detail all the activities you were involved in yesterday, if you're like me you begin at the start of the day and "walk" yourself through the locations to remember what you did at each place. Then, if I ask you what you had for lunch yesterday, you probably catch an image of yourself in situ over your food. Perhaps you were at your kitchen table, at your work station or in a café or restaurant. Even if you ate on the move, you'd probably picture yourself wherever you were, walking and simultaneously munching. From this reference point – whichever it is – you'd work backwards and recall what you were eating. Job done.

Places provide anchors for our memories – they are the reference points by which we plot our movement through time. I believe that without these, our thought processes and specifically our memories would be far more chaotic, random and impossible to recapture. If I'm asked to give an overview of my life, I plot my movements through all the different towns and villages I've lived in. To reveal my experiences with education, I recall first the images of the different schools I went to. For my career, I start by picturing myself in each of the buildings where I have worked.

The three keys to developing a highly efficient memory are Association, Location and Imagination (think of Mohammad ALI to help you remember them) – and once I'd devised the Journey Method, I'd finally arrived at the ultimate solution to the challenge I'd set myself when I first saw Creighton Carvello memorize that deck of cards on TV.

How does it work?

I've told you about how I used the Journey Method to memorize my first deck of cards, but to introduce you to using the method yourself I want to take you specifically through my thought processes as I use a short, seven-stage journey around a typical home to memorize a list of items.

Here are the first seven stages on my Home Journey:

STAGE 1	**Bedroom window**
STAGE 2	**Bedside table**
STAGE 3	**Landing**
STAGE 4	**Bathroom**
STAGE 5	**Linen cupboard**
STAGE 6	**Living room**
STAGE 7	**Kitchen**

First, picture yourself walking the journey in logical steps. Don't worry if this route doesn't exactly match your own home. You can adapt the method to fit your house later on in the process. For now, learn this route so that you can walk it in your mind's eye

INSIDE MY MIND: IT'S ALL GREEK!

When, during my trials with playing cards, I came to the conclusion that using a journey was the most effective way to memorize a list of information, I thought I had developed a new system all of my own. Some years later it came as a bit of a blow to discover that this method was actually thousands of years old! In oral traditions the world over, elders told stories to preserve their customs and cultures for future generations. It turned out that, with papyrus for writing in scarce supply, the ancient Greeks had been using "loci" (places) as an aide-mémoire considerably before I discovered it! So, how did they come up with the system?

The story goes that the ancient Greek poet Simonides of Ceos (c.556– c.468BC) narrowly escaped death when he was called away from a victory banquet to meet two young men outside the palace. When he arrived outside, Simonides couldn't find his visitors, and turned to go back to the feast. However, as he did so an earthquake struck and the banqueting hall collapsed, killing the guests inside. Later, Simonides was asked to identify the bodies of the other diners, which he did by recalling who had been sitting where at the table. Historians claim that this was the birth of the system of memory loci. From then on ancient Greek orators placed elements of their stories at certain places along a mental route in order to recall the story in the right order.

While I have to admit I was a bit shocked to discover that I wasn't even close to being the first person ever to use such a system, I was also reassured – if a system like the Journey Method had been good enough for the ancient Greeks, I must have struck gold.

backwards and forwards. Once you're confident you can do this, you're ready to use it as a set of hooks for a list of seven items. Again, we've talked about how people are easier to hook on to journey stages than objects, but objects provide good test cases while you're getting used to the method (you're also more likely, in your daily life, to want to memorize objects – in the form of shopping lists, or perhaps gifts given to you on your birthday so that you can write thank-you notes).

As strange as it may sound, I recommend that you don't approach this exercise with the intention of making lots of effort to memorize the items. The whole magic of the Journey Method is that it's virtually effortless – you don't have to try too hard, because your powerful imagination and skill at making associations along the familiar journey will result in you automatically recalling the items in their original sequence. Don't forget to hold on to your first associations, which are the ones most likely to come back to you. Here are your items:

FEATHER • TEASPOON • DECKCHAIR • SNAIL • UMBRELLA • ROSES • HAMMOCK

STAGE 1
Bedroom window/Feather
The image that springs to my mind is of a white feather that slowly zigzags down past the bedroom window. Try to make sense of what you imagine to make this image stick. Think of a logical reason why the feather would be floating past – perhaps a bird has dropped it, or the wind has blown it from a nest in your

guttering; or perhaps it is blowing out of your bedroom window, having come free from your feather duvet or pillow. Choose the association that feels most natural and logical to you.

STAGE 2
Bedside table/Teaspoon

At stage 2, I see a teaspoon on the bedside table. That's pretty straightforward, so to help the image stick, I have to ask why it's there. Perhaps it's been left behind from the morning cup of tea, or maybe it was left there after I took a nighttime dose of medicine? Remember how important it is to use your senses to firm up your associations (see p.26)? I want to imagine that I lick the teaspoon, hoping the taste on it will give me a clue as to why it's there and what it has been used for. I fully immerse myself in the scenario.

STAGE 3
Landing/Deckchair

As I move out to the landing, I find a deckchair blocking my path. There's lots of opportunity here to use your senses. What colour is the chair? Is its frame wooden or metal and is it smooth or rough? Do you have to step around the chair or do you have to lift it to move it out of the way? I also ask myself why would someone have left it there? Were they waiting to put it back in the loft? Perhaps a child brought it upstairs to play with it? See yourself sidestepping the chair or collapsing it – remember you're the star of your mind-movie, so do what seems natural. Perhaps you feel a bit agitated or frustrated about the obstruction – all the better if you can use your emotions to make the scene feel more real.

Remember that if you're actually part of the action, you're more likely to trick your brain into thinking it's really happened (see pp.39–40).

STAGE 4
Bathroom/Snail

This stage poses slightly more problems, because a clear line of logic is harder to find. However, this just means that it's time to make one of those associations you practised in Chapter 6. Are there snails all over the bathtub, up the walls, and over the basin? Or can you just see a single snail that's left trails of silvery slime across the tiles on the floor? Perhaps there's only one snail but it's huge and oversized? Personally, I find that exaggerating size interferes with my need for logic and unnecessarily increases the workload on my brain, so I'd probably go for something more believable (the slime trails, perhaps).

STAGE 5
Linen cupboard/Umbrella

Any cupboard on my journeys simply has to be opened! I imagine myself pulling back the door and a bright red umbrella falling out. The colour is important in the process of memorization because it makes the association more vivid. I also try to conjure up the sound of the umbrella as it clunks awkwardly to the floor. Why was the umbrella in the cupboard in the first place? Is it closed or open? Is it a type that's small and compact or is it a large umbrella with a long handle? Who does it belong to? Do you pick it up to put it back?

STAGE 6

Living room/Roses

This room smells of fragrant roses. On top of the coffee table is a vase bursting with bright yellow blooms. You can make them any colour you like. I chose yellow as it's a happy colour – this is how the recipient of the roses may have felt when she or he received them. Why were they given? Perhaps they're a birthday gift?

STAGE 7

Kitchen/Hammock

When I can't find any obvious sense to an association, I put myself inside the scene. I picture a hammock hanging from kitchen-cupboard handles, blocking the path to the back door. I throw myself into the hammock and imagine swinging from side to side and bumping into the refrigerator in the process.

Your journey is complete, and now I bet that you'll be able to answer the following questions with ease (and then certainly by replaying the scene in your head until you come to the answer):

• What item was in the bathroom?
• Where were the roses?
• What is the fourth item on the list?
• Which item is between the feather and the snail?
• Can you name all seven items in order?

Now try the exercise on the following pages, and then read the conclusion on page 62.

EXERCISE 6: Your First Journey

Now it's time for you to test the Journey Method for yourself – this time I won't put ideas into your head, because your own associations will be much stronger than links that I make for you. Follow the steps and as always try not to edit the first links that come to you, but do try to make them as vivid as possible, using all your senses.

1   Devise a route around your house consisting of 12 stages. If you run out of indoor places, extend the journey through your garden and along the road. Make sure the route is logical – don't make stage 1 the bedroom, stage 2 the kitchen and stage 3 your en suite, for example. Second, don't return to a room once you've left it. Write down the list of stages if it helps you to plan your journey – this is what I did when I first developed my own routes back in 1987.

2   Run through the journey in your mind over and over until you can recall it forwards and backwards without thinking. It may help to actually walk the journey a few times, too, if it's practical to do so.

3   Once you're confident you know your journey inside out, apply the Journey Method to memorize the following list of 12 items in the correct order. Allow your vivid imagination to come out to play – remember, use logic and creativity and your senses and emotions. As you move along the route, don't be tempted to look back over the list to refresh your memory. Trust the power of your mind and have faith

that the journey will preserve the items and their order. Take as long as you need, but usually a couple of minutes is enough.

CAKE • HORSE • NEWSPAPER • KETTLE • WHIP • CANNON • BANANA • TELEPHONE • ELVIS PRESLEY • TELESCOPE • BELL • COFFEE

4 Now, cover the list and see how many items you can recall in the exact order. Write the items down. Some will come back to you more easily than others. For example, Elvis Presley was probably one of the easy ones – remember how I discovered that people work far better with the Journey Method than objects, which is why I turned all my playing cards into people? A score of nine or more items is very good.

5 Now, to prove to yourself the thoroughness of the method, answer the following test questions:

• Which item on the list is between Elvis and the bell?
• Which is the third item on the list?
• Which number position on the list is the cannon?
• Which item follows the banana?
• How many items can you recall correctly in reverse order?

Recalling the items in reverse is a toughie. So, congratulations if you got all 12 right. Don't worry if you didn't – it will get easier with practice.

Conclusion: Demystifying the magic

Here's another question for you. Which of the following functions of the left and right hemispheres of your brain have you used for the practical elements of this chapter? And how many of your senses did you use? The answer is – the lot!

Thanks to your left brain, you used sequence, logic, speech, analysis and numeracy (for example, to work out which was the fourth item on the list on page 59), while your right brain gave you imagination, colour, dimension (the size and shape of the objects) and spatial awareness (a sense of location and place). Your senses gave you taste, touch, sight, smell and sound. The two sides of your brain and your senses were all working in harmony.

The exercise on the previous pages is one of the most important in this book, because for the first time you're devising your own journey and using it to memorize a list of items I've given you. I can tell you everything I know, think or have discovered about the Journey Method, but until you start using it for yourself, including devising your own journeys, it will still be an abstract principle that has no bearing on your ability to memorize day to day. I love this bit in the tutoring process, because it's now that everything I've tried to explain so far comes together and you can see for yourself the magic of the Journey Method.

CHAPTER ELEVEN

EVIDENCE FOR THE JOURNEY METHOD

So far, everything I've taught you about the Journey Method suggests that for the best results you use a journey that you know – a real one – to hook items onto. But is there any scientific basis for this? Does repeated use of these journeys in itself make your memory better? And why are real journeys so effective?

In 2002, along with nine other "superior memorizers", I took part in a study conducted by the Institute of Neurology in London to see what happens in our brains as we memorize information.

We underwent Functional Magnetic Resonance Imaging (FMRI): in turn, each of us had brain scans, first to look for anything unusual or irregular in our brains' structure and, second, to see what happened as we committed information to memory. Our results were measured against a control group who had no knowledge of memory techniques. The study concluded that there was nothing genius-like about our brains – structurally, all the "superior memorizers" have brains just like everyone else's.

However, the evidence also showed that when we mnemonists memorize information, we use "spatial learning strategy". This means that we use the region in our brains, the hippocampus, that is especially important for spatial memory (actually, there are two *hippocampi*, but in speech we tend to refer to them collectively as simply the hippocampus). This is the part of the memory that we all use to record information about our surroundings and to orient ourselves within a space, whether it's a room, a building, a park or a city. In essence, the hippocampus helps us not to get lost! The scientific evidence for this makes the efficacy of the Journey Method easier to understand.

When I memorize hundreds of words, numbers or playing cards, I navigate routes around familiar golf courses, holiday locations, towns, villages, friends' houses and gardens, and favourite walks. Every time I do this, I activate my hippocampal region, which gets stronger, in turn strengthening my overall memory. One body of research shows that the hippocampus region of London black cab drivers, who spend three years learning "The Knowledge", about 500 routes around the city, tends to be slightly larger than that of the rest of the population. The more experienced the driver, the bigger the hippocampus. I believe that this is a direct result of having a job that requires hours of navigation. It's really no different from the principle that if you want to have a flatter stomach, you need to exercise your abdominal muscles regularly.

Sense of place and episodic memory

When I stand in a place I know extremely well, such as my kitchen, I attach so many personal memories to it that I can perceive that room in a number of different ways. It's almost as though the room can look completely different depending on the particular memories I conjure up. If you're in a place you've known well for several years, look around you. Now try to recall the image of yourself in the same place, but at an earlier time in your life, or even just on a different day. Does the space feel any different?

When I think about a certain place in relation to a certain memory, the place itself is reinvented according to the mood of that recollection. I believe that our sense of place is tied up not only with our spatial awareness, but also with our episodic memory – the part of the memory that records events that we've been involved in. Your episodic memory is your internal autobiography. When a place holds a chapter (or, even better, chapters) of that story for you, your memory or memories of it, and therefore its efficacy as a memory tool, are very strong.

Ever the investigator, I have been curious to know whether I can simulate this kind of connection to a place. So, using gaming software to help me, I've experimented using virtual reality worlds to develop invented routes for memorizing information. I've even used them in memory competitions. Although I can still get a sense of place from them, I find that the virtual journeys are not as effective as real ones. Somehow my brain is not entirely convinced by them. The conclusion, then, is simple: the most successful routes are those that carry a rich supply of episodic memories and provide strong spatial orientation. This means that the most familiar locations usually provide the best journeys for the Journey Method.

The Von Restorff Effect

However, sense of place is not the only thing that makes the Journey Method work. Its efficacy is also tightly bound up with

INSIDE MY MIND: STAYING SWITCHED ON

I try to arrange my Journey Method routes so that I walk in and out of buildings. I find that this natural flow to and from buildings keeps my attention, while the stages on the journey are posted both inside and outside to keep things fresh for my memory. The regular changes of atmosphere act like small impulses or nudges that prevent me from losing my concentration or becoming complacent. For example, in my original journey from my front gate around the village where I lived, I find myself moving in and out of shops. When I visit the travel agent, I can "feel" the warm, slightly stuffy air on my face, but as soon as I imagine myself moving outside again, I "feel" fresh air on my face and it sort of wakes me up mentally – just as it might in real life. Again, this is all part of the idea of tricking the brain into believing that what I'm imagining has really happened to me.

the way in which we attach images to each of the journeys. In 1933, the German psychologist Hedwig von Restorff conducted a series of experiments to try to identify what makes something memorable. She concluded that one of the strongest criteria for recall is individuality. If something stands out for being a different shape, size, colour or in some other way significantly, characteristically different from the other items around it, it becomes easier to recall. For example, in a field of red poppies, a single sunflower becomes memorable; in a roomful of people dressed in black tie, the person in white tie sticks in the mind. The effect works in reality and also in the abstract. So, take the list Lantern, Stirrup, Fish, Clock, Ears, Vase, Johnny Depp, Car, Necklace, Wheelbarrow, Suitcase, Boat, Hammer, Spoon. The item that stands out is Johnny Depp – not because he's famous, but because he's the only person in a list of inanimate objects.

The Von Restorff Effect is another reason that the Journey Method is so powerful: every item in the list is made exceptional or unusual in some way by its association with the stages on the journey. Let's say, for example, that the item "boat" coincides with the stage of my journey represented by the local cenotaph. I imagine a huge war boat (which makes a logical link between the boat and the war memorial) balancing on top of the monument – it's precariously placed and wobbly, making me anxious that it's going to topple off. The item "boat" is in this way transformed into something exceptional and, therefore, according to the Von Restorff Effect, more memorable. In short, it doesn't matter how dull or uniform a list of items appears at first glance – using the Journey Method transforms the items into subjects that are especially easy to memorize.

CHAPTER TWELVE

TOP 5 TIPS FOR CREATING A MEMORY JOURNEY BANK

I think it would be fair to say that I have a compulsive personality. The Journey Method had given me the means by which to memorize a deck of cards just like Creighton Carvello. However, I'd also by then seen Creighton Carvello's name in the *Guinness World Records* book for memorizing six decks of cards. If I could match his single-deck feat, then surely I, too, could memorize six decks or more and get my own name into print. In other words, once I'd created the Journey Method, I clearly wasn't going to rest until I'd beaten Carvello's record. All I needed to do was to increase the number of routes I used so that I could deal with multiple decks. For example, to memorize six decks of shuffled cards I needed six routes each of 52 stages. Easy!

Within three or four hours I'd managed to master routes around three golf courses, two of my childhood houses and the town of Hastings in East Sussex, where I once worked. (Incidentally, if you're not a golfer, you may have been wondering how three golf courses can be distinctive enough to provide good routes for memorization. I don't really have an explanation for that, except to say that if you *are* a golfer, you'll understand! Each course has its idiosyncratic stops and undulations, and if you play them enough – as I confess I once did – each is wonderfully unique.) I used these routes to memorize six decks of cards – with no errors.

My repeated attempts to refine the system with the goal of getting into the record books, apart from proving to myself that I could be the best, made me realize that in order to achieve great feats of memorization I needed to have a bank of journeys that I could draw upon at will. Over the years I've not only refined and perfected the Journey Method, I've also added to the bank of journeys I use. At first, while I was developing the system and then during the years when I competed at the World Memory Championships, I added several new routes a year, but since I took a break from competition, I've added maybe one 52-stage route annually. Now, I have a collection of 70 routes each of 52 stages that I use again and again. Some I reserve exclusively to tag together to memorize massive amounts of data in competitions; some I save for specific tasks, such as to memorize a to-do list, or the key points of a presentation.

To give you an idea of the sorts of locations I choose, my top 20 routes – that is, the routes that I know best and that have proved most successful for memorization – comprise three golf courses, six houses, five hotels, three towns, two schools and a church. These are all places that I know really well and they already have a memory footprint in my mind. I number them from one to 20 and if I need to use more than one of them for a particular memorization, I always use them in the same order, from one to

INSIDE MY MIND: MAKING THE RECORD BOOKS

Even once I had my bank of journeys, getting my name into print didn't happen overnight. My first attempt to make the record books was in 1988, when I memorized six decks shuffled into each other with only a single sighting of each card. I made no errors ... but then later that year fellow Brit Jonathan Hancock topped me by memorizing seven decks.

More determined than ever, on June 11, 1989, I memorized 25 decks with four errors, but even that wasn't enough. And then, finally, on July 22, 1990, I did it. I memorized 35 decks of cards with only two errors and entered the Guinness World Records *book (1991 edition).*

I can remember being on holiday and rushing into a shop to buy a copy of the book on its launch day. My excitement was at an all-time high. This was going to change my life! More important, though, was that seeing my name in print confirmed in my own mind that perhaps I wasn't as empty-headed as I'd always been told I was at school. With self-confidence and determination, perhaps there was nothing that my memory couldn't achieve.

Today, although that original record has been broken, I've had several other entries in Guinness. My journeys are so much second nature to me now that not only have I made the record books for numbers of cards memorized, but also for the speed of my memorizations. In 1996, on the UK show Recordbreakers, *I memorized a single deck in just 38.29 seconds and, in fact, I hold the current world record for number of cards memorized: 54 decks, following a single sighting of each card, with only eight errors, which I achieved in May 2002.*

20. There are no hard-and-fast rules for deciding which locations will make your best memory journeys – choosing the journeys you'll use to store information is entirely a personal matter, but I do have some top tips that I hope will help to make your own memory journey bank a truly successful one.

1 Choose routes that you know inside out

Apart from enabling you to concentrate on the items you need to memorize, rather than on the route of the journey itself, knowing the journey seamlessly is one of the keys to shaving off seconds in the process of memorization (and it's the reason that I've made the record books for speed; see box, opposite). Forest walks I often take with my dog, homes I've lived in, towns and villages I've lived in for years, and so on, all provide me with perfect journey material. I know all my journeys so well – forwards and backwards – that travelling from one stop to the next has become virtually automatic. Instead of mentally watching myself walk step after step along the journey, I appear to travel in a series of snapshots – it's like a slideshow in my mind. However, don't expect this to happen immediately. When you start out, you might need to "walk" your way through your journeys, but eventually you'll be able to zip magically from one place to another – as long as your journeys are second nature to you.

2 Choose routes that have significance for you

This is connected to the first top tip, but it's important enough to warrant a mention of its own. When I start a memorization, I place myself at the first stop on my journey and I take a few seconds to get a sense of where I am. I soak up the atmosphere around me, and I slip back in time to try to recapture the emotions I felt in that place. In effect, I trick my brain into believing that I'm there again, standing at that very place – the more real I can make it, the more likely it is that my memorizations will stick. Journeys that take you to places that have or have had meaning in your life, so that they are rich with emotion and significance, will make the best journeys for successful memorization. Many of my favourite journeys are set within places where I've felt particularly happy.

3 Choose journeys that give good variety

Design your routes so that the stops are varied and interesting and appear in a variety of locations. I often have students who think that a familiar train journey makes a great memory journey. However, they soon find that once they've stopped at three or four stations, the route itself can become complicated to remember – after a while, one train station begins to look like another.

I once set a group of students the challenge of memorizing the main stories on each page of a newspaper. Using their initial routes, the students struggled to recall more than the first three or four headlines – and then I showed them how more interesting journeys would dramatically improve their recall. I was running the course in a castle, which made a fantastic setting for a series of interesting stops – so, taking to our feet, we actually walked a route and memorized as we went along. We discussed the first headline in the lecture room; then we moved to another room with a table that had a chess set laid out on it and there we reviewed page two. In the dining room, I showed everyone photos and stories from the third page. Our journey took us around the castle, into the garden – at each stage reviewing the next page in the newspaper – until finally we came to the car park where we looked at and talked about the last page. When we returned to the lecture room, to everyone's delight, by mentally walking the route the group recalled one or more items of news from every page.

In and out of rooms and buildings, and across paths, rivers and fields, each journey in your bank should have stages that are as distinct from one another as possible. Changes of scenery and transitions between inside and outside keep me alert and focused and stop me becoming complacent about where I am.

4 Choose certain journeys to memorize certain things

I find that some journeys work better in the memorization of specific things. For example, generally I find journeys based on open spaces are ideal for memorizing speeches and names. To memorize a speech I use the layout of a golf course. It's a personal thing, but I feel less restricted using outside locations for speeches – I have plenty of space to lay down mnemonic images, some of which might be complicated and require several associations in one place (for example, if I have a quotation to memorize). Similarly, I use one of my favourite countryside walks to memorize names, because some names, particularly those with three or four syllables, require me to link together several images (which all have to be stored at one stop) for just that one piece of information. If I have lots of space around each stop in my journey, I have space to place the combination of images without them feeling confined, awkward or illogical.

On the other hand, when I memorize playing cards, I use one image per playing card (or pair of playing cards – more of this later), and I use one image for pairs of numbers (again, we'll come to this). So, for playing cards and numbers, interior settings, where a single image can be attached to a single position, work perfectly well. Of course, such choices are deeply personal – you'll know what works best for you.

5 Choose journeys that give good vantage points

Every time I travel a journey, I see the snapshot of each place from exactly the same vantage point I have always used. For example, when I arrive at the travel agent stop on one of my journeys, I always stand just inside the door looking at the adverts on the wall; when I arrive at the level crossing, I always stand in the middle of it, looking up the road. I peer through the window of the clothes shop – I never go inside to look out. Consistency in the viewpoints each time I use a particular journey speeds up the process of moving from stage to stage, so it's important that your chosen journeys provide stages that have good, instinctive vantage points, so that you don't find yourself wanting to change them each time you use that route.

CHAPTER THIRTEEN

SPINNING THE MEMORY PLATES

I've talked a lot about the vast number of items I can memorize in a single sitting, and I've probably made it sound as though I do this at a first attempt, without going back at all during the memorization to check what I've already implanted in my brain. However, it's not quite that simple (or superhuman!). When I take part in my record-breaking memory attempts, I recognize that I have a limit beyond which the first items in a memorized sequence can start to become a bit hazy. It's vital, therefore, to have time for review. Knowing when and how many times to review the data you need to remember (whether that's decks of cards or a shopping list or information for a meeting or exam) will make the difference between success and failure in your attempts at recall.

A good analogy is the circus act of plate spinning. The performer spins plates on the ends of upright sticks, one at a time. After about ten or so of these plates have been set up to spin, the first two or three start to wobble. The performer checks these first few plates, gives the sticks a bit of a spin to keep the plates going, and then continues to spin more and more plates until there are 30 or more whirling away at the same time.

When I memorize data, a similar thing happens. I can begin memorizing, say, several decks of cards, sequences of numbers, peoples' names and so on, but at some point – you'll learn what point that is for you simply through trial, error and experience – the ones I memorized at the beginning start to wobble in my head. And that's why, if you want a perfect memory, you have to learn an effective method of review.

The Rule of Five

If I have a limited amount of time to memorize a large amount of data, I know that I need to be able to review it five times for that information to stick. The more reviews I have, the stronger the retention and the longer I can store the memories, but if time is short, such as during a competition or if I have to memorize a series of names in a room quickly, five reviews is the minimum.

In 2002, I made the record books by memorizing 54 decks of playing cards, shuffled randomly into one another. At some point in my future, I intend to annihilate my own record and memorize a sequence of 100 decks. Someone will shuffle all 5,200 cards into each other and then divide them up again into 100 piles of 52, set face down on a table. I will then attempt to memorize the entire sequence by looking at each card just once. At the end of the memorization, I'll attempt to recall the sequence. According to the strict rules of the *Guinness World Records*, I'm allowed only a half of one-percent margin of error. This means I can make no more than 26 mistakes in total.

This may sound like an impossible challenge, but actually the memorization of each deck of 52 cards is far from impossible.

First, I am utterly confident that my system works. I can have 100 well-prepared 52-stage journeys and, using the Journey Method, I know I'll be able to place one card at each stage of a journey, in order, and make it stick until I've used all the journeys and memorized all the cards. (In practice, these days I have a shortcut that enables me to place two cards at each stage, but I want to keep things simple for now, so I'll explain the shortcut later.)

In fact, whether or not I succeed will not really be down to my ability to apply the Journey Method, but instead it will be down to the effectiveness of my review strategy – that is, my application of the Rule of Five.

Once I've memorized the first pile of 52 cards (which takes about three minutes), I'll immediately carry out my first review of that sequence. The review takes about 30 seconds. As this is a single-sighting challenge, I won't be able to look again at the cards, so I'll review the cards from memory alone by mentally walking the route again. I'll do the same for the next four piles – memorizing and then reviewing from memory each sequence along its journey.

When I've memorized and reviewed the first five piles, I'll start my second review. For this, I'll review the cards in all five piles from beginning to end. Only once I've done that will I start memorizing the next batch of five piles of cards, again with a first review of each pile of 52, followed by a second review of that entire set of five piles. Once I've memorized 25 piles of cards (a mere quarter of the total!), doing first and second reviews in groups of five, I'll begin my third review – starting at the first card of the first pile and ending with the last card of the 25th pile, in sequence. I'll take my fourth review after I've completed the next

25 piles (each of these undergoing the same process of review as the first 25 piles) – so I'll mentally review all the cards from 50 piles. At this point I should be fairly confident that I can recall the order of the first 2,600 cards without error. In that case I'll repeat the whole exercise all over again for the remaining 50 piles.

Finally, I'll carry out my fifth and final review only after I have memorized all 100 decks. Once I've completed my fifth review, I'll attempt to recall the entire sequence of 5,200 cards, reciting them one by one. I estimate that to recall and recite each of the cards alone will take me approximately six hours.

My Rule of Five system for 100 decks might be easier to follow with the help of this diagram:

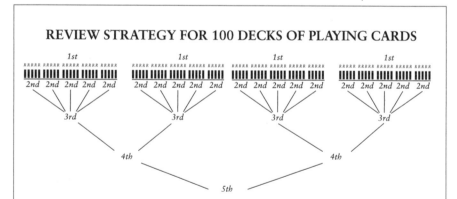

REVIEW STRATEGY FOR 100 DECKS OF PLAYING CARDS

1st, 2nd, 3rd, 4th and 5th refer to the stages of review. You review each of the first five decks in turn, separately, immediately after memorizing the cards in each deck. Then after completing your 1st review of the fifth deck, you do your 2nd review of all five decks together. Then you move on to memorize and review the next 5 decks in the same way; and continue doing 1st and 2nd reviews until you have memorized 25 decks. At this point you do a 3rd review of all 25 x 52 cards. Then you follow then same procedure for the next 25 decks, and then do a 4th review ... and so on until your 5th review.

I believe that this pattern of reviewing has been crucial to my winning eight World Memory Championships titles. During competition, entrants are given a certain amount of time for memorizing and then a certain amount of time for recall. I have been in competitions in which as soon as the clock starts for the recall time, most of the competitors immediately begin to scribble down their memorized sequences as fast as they can. They worry that the information will quickly start to fade from their memory. Maybe only two or three competitors, myself included, sit quietly to use this critical time for one final mental review.

Whatever the discipline, whether I have just memorized names and faces, thousands of binary digits or hundreds of words, the first thing I do before attempting to recall anything is carry out an immediate review. I have to confess, though, I don't always review five times – sometimes, particularly in competition, I just don't have time. Nevertheless, five reviews is the number I believe to be the optimum for perfect memorization, so I try to stick by my Rule of Five as much as I can.

The next time you're at a party and you're introduced to people you've never met before, or your partner rattles through a list of items you need to buy at the store, or you're boss gives you a spoken list of instructions, try using the principles of the Rule of Five. As soon as you've been given the pieces of information (names, items or instructions), repeat the complete list to yourself in your head (if you're memorizing names, you might be able to repeat them back aloud to the appropriate people). If you've been given a shopping list or instructions, don't be tempted to hurry off and write anything down, simply make an immediate

INSIDE MY MIND: SPOTTING THE COMPETITION

In 1998, at the German Memory Championships, the bell sounded for the recall phase of the various disciplines and, each time, most people frantically began to write. However, I spotted one competitor who sat quietly with his eyes closed. Whether the discipline involved cards, numbers or words, he was obviously reviewing his memorization one final time. At that moment I knew this man was a threat – if he was practising a review strategy, he could strip me of my World Championship crown. His name was Dr Gunther Karsten, and not only did he go on to win the German Championships eight times, he finally secured the World title in 2007. He, too, uses the Journey Method – and he practises the art of review – although to what extent, I may never know!

review in your mind. Then, a few minutes later make another mental review – all the time remaining calm. You may need to review only once or twice – the number of reviews will differ according to the amount of information you need to memorize. The important thing is the immediacy of the reviews. If, instead of reviewing straightaway, you waited as you frantically tried to find a pen and paper to write down the information, you'd have wasted precious time (if you can't recall it immediately, then it's unlikely you'll recall it once you've found a pen and paper). If you review straightaway, there's no slippage because no time is lost before you embed the information in your memory.

CHAPTER FOURTEEN

FROM CARDS
TO NUMBERS

Soon after I'd mastered the art of card memorization, I wondered if I could transfer this skill to memorizing long sequences of numbers. Our lives are governed by numbers. Telephone numbers, transport timetables, weights and measures, population statistics, election results, PINs, entry codes and numerical passwords – to name a few. Even if you don't want to attempt the numerical challenges I encounter during competitions, everything has to be quantified, tallied, reckoned, and made secure – so being able to memorize numbers counts!

Psychologists have determined that, on average, the human brain can retain around only seven to nine pieces of data in its short-term (working) memory. This assessment may be accurate, but it's certainly not insuperable. Using my memory systems, I've shown that it's possible to memorize far more than nine digits (in fact, I've memorized well into the hundreds!) at a time, as long as you have a strategy for doing it.

Some people, mathematicians mostly, see real beauty in numbers. I'm sad to say that as I was growing up I wasn't one of these enlightened folk. Until I started to perform feats of memorization, sequences of numbers to me seemed unintelligible and instantly forgettable. However, *now* when I look at a series of numbers, they appear completely differently to me. They come to life; they are animated, colourful and even at times humorous. Now, numbers have characters all of their own. Why? Because I have developed a way to convert them from (to me at least) their normal, dull, meaningless form into something that my brain can work with.

The secret to memorizing numbers is to attach significance to them by translating them into coded images. This lies at the heart of a strategy I call my "language of numbers".

However, there are several simpler systems that people use, so I want to start by teaching you these. For short number sequences, such as memorizing a PIN, they come in pretty handy.

Number–shapes

Have you ever looked at the shape of the number "2" and thought that it resembles a swan? Or at "4" and seen the sail of a boat or perhaps a flag on a pole? The number–shape system works on the principle that we can translate any number into an image according to its unique from. As a quick experiment, using a pen and paper, write down the first image that enters your mind as you think of each number form zero to nine. Write down the numbers first, if it helps you. Compare your ideas with mine, which appear in the box on the opposite page (but remember that your own associations will always be stronger for you). I've included drawings of some of the associations to make it clearer how the system works.

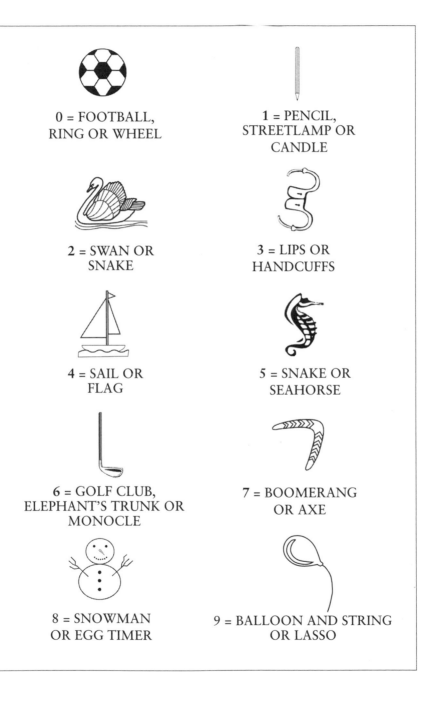

0 = FOOTBALL,
RING OR WHEEL

1 = PENCIL,
STREETLAMP OR
CANDLE

2 = SWAN OR
SNAKE

3 = LIPS OR
HANDCUFFS

4 = SAIL OR
FLAG

5 = SNAKE OR
SEAHORSE

6 = GOLF CLUB,
ELEPHANT'S TRUNK OR
MONOCLE

7 = BOOMERANG
OR AXE

8 = SNOWMAN
OR EGG TIMER

9 = BALLOON AND STRING
OR LASSO

As there are only ten digits to translate to images, this is a very simple code to learn. Once you're able to see a number as an object, you can use the object codes to memorize short sequences of numbers by using the objects as elements of a story.

For example, take the number 1 7 9 2, which was the number of steps in the Eiffel Tower when it first opened. Using my number–shape associations, you might picture yourself in Paris at night time, holding a candle (the number–shape for one). Carrying the candle, you head toward the Eiffel Tower. At the entrance you notice a man chopping away at one of the steel legs, using an axe (the number–shape for seven). The futility of this activity makes it all the more memorable. You begin your ascent of the tower steps. When you reach the top, someone hands you a balloon on a string (the number–shape for nine). Give the balloon a colour to make it more memorable – mine is red. As you gaze across Paris, the full moon glows in the night sky and you see the silhouette of a swan – which gives you your number–shape for two – fly across the moon's face.

Anchoring your story to a location that's relevant to the number you're trying to remember is another important aide-mémoire. If you needed to remember your credit card or debit account PIN, a short route around your local bank or from your house to the bank would be perfect.

Number–rhymes

If number–shapes don't appeal to you, you could try number–rhymes. This time the image you form to represent the number rhymes with the number sound. So, for one you could have bun, for two, shoe, and so on. Again, create the rhymes that are most natural to you, but I imagine they'll be quite similar to mine:

0 = HERO, NERO (THE ROMAN EMPEROR)
1 = BUN, SUN
2 = SHOE, GLUE
3 = TREE, SEA
4 = DOOR, BOAR
5 = HIVE, CHIVE
6 = STICKS, BRICKS
7 = HEAVEN (OR PERHAPS KEVIN, IF YOU'VE GOT A
       FRIEND WITH THAT NAME)
8 = GATE, WEIGHT
9 = WINE, PINE

Let's say you're visiting a friend without your car. Your friend tells you that you need to catch the number 839 bus, which stops right outside her house. How could you use the number–rhyme system to remember which bus to catch? Imagine that the bus pulls up at the bus stop. To get on it, you have to open a gate (eight). The first person you see on the bus, sitting in the front row of seats, is holding a small tree (three) in a tub on her lap, as you pass her you notice that the tree is a pine (nine) – perhaps it has Christmas decorations on it to make the pine-tree image more vivid. If you review the scene a couple of times, you won't forget which bus you're supposed to be on.

Quick, easy and practical for short sequences of numbers, number–shapes and number–rhymes find their way into my everyday memorizations all the time. However, these systems are not developed enough to help me in World Memory Championships, so I've had to devise my own.

Memorizing pi

Creighton Carvello, who had inspired me to memorize cards in the first place, had managed to memorize pi (the area of a circle, divided by the square of its radius) to 20,013 decimal places. Pi is an infinite number which, as far as we know, doesn't repeat itself. Consequently, it makes for an excellent measure of a person's memory capacity. It won't surprise you to know then, that pi was the next challenge I set for myself.

Over the years, my experimentation with memory techniques has taught me several things about the best way to make information stick, one of them being that letters are easier to turn into usable codes than numbers.

In the early days of my experimentation, I set about coding numbers in exactly the same way as I had coded playing cards: by turning them into letters and then into images. I developed a system for memorizing groups of five numbers, each as a single image. So how does this work for memorizing the decimal places of pi? The first 30 decimal places of pi look like this:

[3.]141592653589793238462643383279

As I studied the first 15 digits, I decided to give each number a specific letter, and to use the letters to form a word or words that I could string into a story. To improve my chances of being able to create a usable sequence of letters, I wrote out the alphabet to U and assigned each number two possible letter codes by running out one to nine twice and then giving 0 the options of S, T and U. The whole thing looked like this:

A	B	C	D	E	F	G	H	I
1	2	3	4	5	6	7	8	9

J	K	L	M	N	O	P	Q
1	2	3	4	5	6	7	8

R	S	T	U
9	0	0	0

So, 1 = A, the first letter of the alphabet, but also J, which is the tenth letter of the alphabet; 2 = B or K; and so on.

Using these number–letter codes 14159 became AMANI, 26535 translated became BONCE, and 89793 translated became HIPIL. If a particular word didn't make sense, then I would break the word down into smaller syllables and therefore more images. For AMANI, I imagined an Indian man (a man I); for BONCE, I imagined a head (bonce being a colloquial word for head, of course), and for HIPIL I pictured a hip with a disease: a hip ill. So far so good, until I looked at the next 15 digits complete with their codes:

23846   26433   83279
BLQDO   BOMCC   QCBPI

These letter sets required quite a bit of creative thinking before I could form some sort of image. So, BLQDO became a block of wood (BLQ) balanced on my own head (DO = Dominic); BOMCC became a bomb (BOM) on a motorbike (CC, as in the engine power of a motorbike) and QCBPI became a barrister (QC) handing a BP (British Petroleum) sign to an Indian man (I). (The images were complicated to come up with, but the best I could think of at the time.)

To remember the numbers in sequence, I created an extended journey from my house leading through the village, the church and its graveyard, over a hill and then into town. I attached the images of each set of five numbers to a stage in the journey, until (with some persistence) I'd laid down a route of 820 stages in a continuous, unbroken journey, each stage representing five numbers of pi. The result was that I could recite pi to 4,100 decimal places.

This was still a long way off Carvello's record, but I could see that, if I persevered, his achievement would be within reach. However, as a task, converting and memorizing pi proved so arduous that I decided to abandon the project and instead worked on refining the number system itself.

Creating a language for numbers

I wanted a system that would allow me to look at numbers and form images almost instantaneously, as if I were reading sentences from a book.

The approach of creating images had worked with playing cards, so why not with numbers, too? And then I realized where my number memorizations had so far been going wrong. Groups of five numbers were too complicated – instead, I should be grouping the numbers into only pairs. As it turned out, as frustrating as learning those few thousand places of pi had been, I'd paved the way for a system that eventually was to help me secure eight World Memory Championships titles – I called it the "Dominic System".

INSIDE MY MIND: TAKING THE POSITIVES

On reflection, it's tempting to think my dalliance with pi had been a complete waste of time. However, although I had lost a couple of weeks memorizing all those numbers, I had gained much from the experience. I realized that there really was no limit to what and how much I could remember, as long as I could find enough places in the world to use as mental storage space. I also learned that the speed with which I could memorize those numbers depended upon the efficiency of the system I used and how much I practised using it.

CHAPTER FIFTEEN

THE DOMINIC SYSTEM

The Dominic System works by assigning a specific letter to each number from zero to nine and then grouping the number–letters in a sequence into pairs. The system is a refinement of the first technique I came up with (to memorize pi), because it simplifies the codes – there's only one possible letter code per number. So:

1 = A	6 = S
2 = B	7 = G
3 = C	8 = H
4 = D	9 = N
5 = E	0 = O

One to five take the letters A to E – the first five letters of the alphabet. Originally, I decided to give all the numbers their corresponding letter of the alphabet – this seemed the most logical approach. However, it wasn't actually the most natural formula for me, so I went with my instinct instead.

I coded six as the letter S, because of its sound. I gave seven the letter G because of the G7 configuration of world finance ministers. Eight takes H for its similar sound, and similarly nine takes N. Zero is coded with the letter O, because of its shape.

Using my new codes and following my realization that pairs of letters were more usable than longer strings of letters, the first 24 places of pi now looked like this:

14	15	92	65	35	89
AD	AE	NB	SE	CE	HN

79	32	38	46	26	43
GN	CB	CH	DS	BS	DC

I knew from my experiences with memorizing playing cards that people (compared with objects) gave me the most reliable images to work with. So, the pairs of letters gave me triggers for names – sometimes the letters represented initials, sometimes they reminded me of shortenings of people's full names. Either way, I could easily translate each pair of numbers into a single person.

The people I chose to represent each pairing were people who had particular significance for me – sometimes because I knew them, sometimes because they were famous (or infamous!). When I scanned the pairs, certain names occurred to me in a flash.

For example, I knew a man at my golf club called Addie – AD (14) immediately makes me think of him. NB (92) makes me think of someone I know called Nobby. I think of my sister-in-law, Henny, when I see HN (89). Filling in a few letters I get Gene for GN (79), Desmond for DS (46) and Dick for DC (43).

For the rest of the numbers I have to use initials: AE (15) gives me Albert Einstein; SE (65) becomes the singer Sheena Easton; and CE (35) are the initials of the actor Clint Eastwood.

Think of a number, any number

There are 100 combinations of number pairings (00, 01, 02 ... all the way up to 97, 98, 99). In order to be able to apply the Dominic System quickly to any sequence of numbers, I needed to have already banked people codes for every pairing. This meant that I needed to dedicate a bit of time to devise a list of 100 characters – one for each possible pair. I'll use my own examples throughout this book, but to be confident about your own memorizations, you may need to write a list of your own number–people codes.

Props, features and actions

I find that my memorizations stick better when each assigned character has a prop, feature or action, too. This helps to cement the character in my mind. For example, I picture Addie (AD/14) swinging a golf club; my sister-in-law Henny (HN/89) is an artist, so I picture her holding a paint brush; and the singer Sheena Easton (SE/65) clutches a microphone.

Putting it all together

Once you're familiar with your cast of characters and are proficient at converting pairs of numbers into them, you can use the Journey Method to memorize long numerical sequences.

Using the layout of a home, this is how you can start to memorize the decimal places of pi. I've started you off below with the first ten decimal places, but how many you get to is limited really only by the length of your journey. If, like me, you can join several journeys together (I often use journeys of 50 stages, in a similar way to the way I memorize cards), then you can easily work into the thousands (remembering that each stop "holds" the codes for two numbers in the sequence). Here's how it works:

STAGE 1	Front door	AD	14
STAGE 2	Kitchen	AE	15
STAGE 3	Utility room	NB	92
STAGE 4	Living room	SE	65
STAGE 5	Stairs	CE	35

At the front door of my house, I picture Addie (AD/14) standing in the doorway swinging his golf club. I shuffle past Addie, trying to avoid his swing, and enter the kitchen, where I see Albert Einstein (AE/15) scribbling a formula on my noticeboard. In the utility room is Nobby (NB/92), and he's strumming the guitar he plays, but he's getting agitated because there's different music coming from the living room. I go in there to see Sheena Easton (SE/65) singing into her microphone. I leave the living room and move to go up the stairs, but on the bottom step is Clint Eastwood, chewing on a cigar and saying "Go ahead. Make my day!"

If I run through these scenes just once more, I know that I have memorized the first ten decimal places of pi. What's more, I can repeat the number backwards as well as forwards by simply reversing the journey through my house and the initials of the person at each stage. (Note that for such a short sequence, it's probably not necessary to apply the Rule of Five; see pp.76–80.)

Now that you know how the Dominic System works, try the exercise on the following pages.

EXERCISE 7: Twenty Numbers

In this exercise the characters and ten-stage journey are up to you. You have 5 minutes for the memorization itself (step 4). Use the questions in step 5 to test the efficacy of your own characters.

1 On a sheet of paper write the numbers 0 to 9. Next to each number designate a letter that makes a logical code for you.

2 Now, look at this 20-digit number:

5 6 6 4 9 2 8 8 2 7 5 3 1 2 2 0 1 5 3 5

Without altering the order of the numbers, split the digits up into pairs, then write each pair down the left-hand side of a sheet of paper.

3 Next to each pair of numbers, make a new column of corresponding letter codes. In a third column give each pair of letter codes its character (using the letters either as initials or because they remind you of a particular name). In a final column, write down each character's action, feature or prop.

4 In your mind's eye, walk yourself through your ten-stop journey. At the first stop, imagine the first character on your list. Don't forget to use their prop, feature or action, too, and add in sensory detail and emotions. Continue to make the mini-movie in your mind, until you have been to all the stops and imagined all the characters. Once

you've finished, do a single review of the characters on the journey – do this from memory, without referring back to the list of characters.

5 Now see how many of these questions you can answer (the more you get right, the more efficient your codes). Note your answers down on a sheet of paper and then refer back to the original sequence to see if you got them all right.

- What is the seventh number in the sequence?
- Which two numbers follow 2 7?
- What are the first six numbers?
- What are the last four numbers?
- How many numbers are there before the first number 3?
- Which two numbers come before the sequence 1 5?
- What is the 13th number in the sequence?
- What are the 11th, 17th and 19th numbers in the sequence?
- Can you note down every third number in the sequence?
- Can you note down the whole sequence in reverse? (Don't worry if you can't – it's your first attempt, after all!)

If you didn't manage to answer all the questions correctly, don't worry. Try the journey again, but attempt to memorize only the first ten numbers in the sequence. Test yourself by writing down the sequence on a sheet of paper. Once you can recall the first ten accurately, try memorizing all 20 again, testing yourself with the questions.

CHAPTER SIXTEEN

DOUBLE PAIRS AND COMPLEX IMAGES

In the last exercise you turned ten pairs of numbers into characters. As I mentioned on page 92, to use the Dominic System quickly, it's best to have converted all 100 possible pairs – and I don't deny that this takes a significant degree of commitment. Learning the entire cast of 100 characters and their associated actions, features and props so that you connect a pair of numbers to a character almost instantly – it's like becoming fluent in a new language – is hugely time-consuming. However, once you've learned this new language, not only can it be put to practical use on a day-to-day basis, but the learning process itself will exercise your brain, improve your levels of concentration and sharpen your memory.

There are ten disciplines at the World Memory Championships. In various guises they involve memorizing numbers, binary digits, playing cards, names and faces, dates, words, and images (see box, opposite, for a full breakdown). One of the most taxing heats is the one-hour Spoken Number round. In this, competitors are required to memorize as many numbers as possible in one hour, which they then must recall in the correct sequence. When I first entered the Championships, I used the method I've just taught

INSIDE MY MIND: CHAMPIONSHIP ROUNDS

The World Memory Championships, which first appeared in 1991, was the brainchild of Tony Buzan (the inventor of Mind Maps®) and Raymond Keene OBE, a chess grandmaster. They believed that people need to exercise their minds in just the same way that they exercise their bodies, and – just as we compete internationally at physical sport – what better way to advance this purpose than to have an international competition that pits the world's greatest mental athletes against one another. I've been involved in the Championships since the beginning as both a competitor and an organizer. In the latter capacity, I have helped to refine the ten rounds that make up the competition, so that they are fair for everyone who competes. The rounds of the Championships are:

Abstract Images • Binary Numbers • One-hour Numbers • Names and Faces • Speed Numbers • Historic and Future Dates • One-hour Cards • Random Words • Spoken Number • Speed Cards

I enjoy all the disciplines, but my favourite is the One-hour Cards because it's a real test of stamina – memorizing 24 decks in an hour really puts me through my paces! The Spoken Number is probably the most gruelling, as it's "sudden death". Although I might attempt to recall 300 digits at the rate of one per second, if haste makes me forget, say, the third digit, my score is just two – which makes this round a test of my nerve, my concentration, and my ability to close my mind to distractions.

you – placing one person (two digits) on each stage of my journey. This system enabled me to memorize 1,000 digits in one hour – and I used it to win the first few Championships. However, as more people took up the sport of memory, not only did the sheer number of competitors increase year after year, but so did their calibre. I realized that I would need to improve on the efficiency of the Dominic System if I were to keep my competitive edge.

So how could I do this? Clearly, I had to squeeze more numbers into each single stage of the journey. If I could somehow double the number of digits at each stage, I would also potentially double the number of single digits I could memorize in an hour. The wonderful thing was that I had the solution to this problem already embedded within the system I was using.

Remember how each character has an action, feature or prop to give him or her some personality? I realized that if I coded the first pair of numbers in the sequence as a character and the second pair as only a prop, feature or action, I could combine the character of the first pair with the prop, feature or action of the second pair, then place that combination of character and, say, action at the first stage of the journey. Then, the third pair (the fifth and sixth numbers) would again be coded as a character and the fourth pair (the seventh and eighth numbers) as a prop and that combination would be placed at the second stage in the journey; and so on. The result was that I would have linked each stage of the journey to four numbers in the sequence.

For example, if I wanted to memorize the number 15562053, I would need to use only two stages in my journey. The first pair of digits (15) gives me AE, or Albert Einstein. The second pair gives me ES, or Edward Scissorhands. So, to memorize the first four digits of this sequence, at the first stop on my journey I imagine Albert Einstein cutting hair – the hair-cutting is Edward Scissorhands' action. Edward doesn't himself appear – instead, Albert Einstein becomes the surrogate for the action that, in the original system, embedded him in my mind. The third pair of digits (20) gives me BO, which for me is Barack Obama (this is one character I've recently updated). The final pair (53) becomes EC, or Eric Clapton, whose action is playing guitar. So, to memorize these four digits, I imagine Barack Obama playing guitar and I place that image at the second stage in my journey. (As a matter of interest, if you reversed the two pairs of digits to give 5320, you'd have Eric Clapton waving a US flag. The system obviously works with any permutation of numbers.)

These characters plus their surrogate props, features or actions are what I call complex images. They are, effectively, interchangeable pieces of a mental jigsaw puzzle, which can be mixed and matched in 10,000 different ways to enable me to memorize vast sequences of numbers in the shortest time possible.

I believe the effort that I put into devising this system kept me ahead of the rest of the competition in the early days – I don't believe that any of my initial rivals had found a system that enabled them so efficiently to memorize four digits at once. Now, however, the story is quite different – competitors these days are becoming more and more adept at number memorization, which means that I'm always looking to make improvements to my system. If nothing else, this certainly keeps me on my toes!

CHAPTER SEVENTEEN

BECOMING CARD SHARP: MULTIPLE DECKS

My work with numbers, and specifically creating complex images (pp.96–9), led the way for me to further hone my skills at memorizing cards. When I started doing this, I was trying to beat Creighton Carvello's record for a single deck. As I mentioned earlier, I soon realized that I had within my grasp the ability to memorize multiple decks. Later on, I realized that I could make that goal more realistic if I could translate the method I was using to memorize long sequences of numbers into an approach or strategy I could use for multiple decks of cards.

You already know the basics of memorizing playing cards (see pp.43–62). I always encourage people to learn a new skill by taking things one step at a time to prevent failure. So, I suggest you feel really confident with placing one card at one stop on a journey *and* with the Dominic System before you try the technique in this chapter. To make this new variation easier once you do begin, though, I've broken it down into small steps so that you have a run of successes – rather than trying to do too much too soon and becoming frustrated. I want you to experiment with a few cards to begin with, just to satisfy yourself that the principle works. If you're successful with a handful of playing cards, this will give you the impetus and the confidence to use it to try to memorize more, and then eventually a whole deck and even perhaps more than one deck.

First steps

You'll need a deck of cards. The first thing you must do with it is pull out the court cards (the Jacks, Queens and Kings) and then arrange them according to suit (Clubs, Diamonds, Hearts and Spades).

Now it's time to bring into play some of the principles you've already learned. At the beginning of the book I said that I associate every card in the deck with a character, and that some of the characters come to me in a flash. Well, one logical way in which I assign characters is to ensure that the suit itself, linked with the value of the specific card, provides a clear and logical connection to the character. Try it. Perhaps the Queen of Diamonds is Queen Elizabeth II of England; and the Queen of Hearts, your wife or girlfriend (or the King of Hearts, your husband or boyfriend). In other words, Diamonds might give characters who are wealthy, while Hearts could be those you love or admire.

Having assigned your characters, you need to integrate one of the elements of the Dominic System. Each of your characters needs a prop, feature or action. So, for example, if Bill Gates is your King of Diamonds, picture him counting bundles of cash or sitting at his laptop checking his latest bank statement. The prop, feature or action animates your characters. In time, it will also help you to memorize longer lists of cards, because you can turn each card into a complex image, just as I do with the long sequences of numbers.

Place the pile of court cards face down in front of you. One by one, turn over each court card. Each time you turn up a new card, look at it, make a character association, give the character an action, and turn the next card. Keep doing this until all the court cards have a character and action and then review the choices you've made, altering them as necessary, until you're happy with the associations and they're firmly embedded in your memory.

Once the cast list for your court cards comes naturally to you, you're ready to shuffle them (still keeping them separate from the rest of the deck) and then memorize them in the new random order. You'll need a 12-stage journey for this. Use one from your journey bank, or invent a new journey. As I've said before, I have journeys that I keep for memorizing cards and numbers (while others work better for names and faces and words; see p.73).

Run through your route a couple of times to familiarize yourself with the stops. Place the pile of shuffled court cards face down in front of you. Turn over the first card. With good preparation, you should instantly recognize it as the character you've given it, and all you need to do is to place that character, including his or her prop, feature or action, at the first stop on your journey.

Let's say the first card you turn over is the King of Hearts and you've given that card the character of your father, and let's say he's a keen tennis player (which gives him his action). If the first stage of your journey is your front gate, you would imagine your dad at your gate practising his serve – perhaps he's serving over the gate into the road, and you flinch as he narrowly misses the cars!

If the next card is the Queen of Diamonds and you've given her the character of Queen Elizabeth II (with the action of knighting someone), you would place her at the second stop in your journey (perhaps your front door). She's motioning to you to kneel as you approach her so that she can knight you.

Spend as long as you need walking through your journey and placing the 12 court cards at the 12 stops. Your aim is to accustom your mind to the conversion process, while also allowing your imagination free rein to bring the cards to life. Your brain is having to do several things at once – see a card, convert it to a character, place the character in the journey, and memorize it. Remember to use emotion and all your senses and to try to make the connections logical so that you aren't asking your brain to work harder than it needs to. Go through the whole 12-card stack again, if you like, and then once you think you have it memorized, review it in your mind without looking at the cards. Then, again without looking at the cards, write down the sequence of cards.

How did you do? Don't be hard on yourself if you made a few mistakes – although do try to work out where you went wrong. If some of the associations weren't strong enough, perhaps it would be better to substitute other characters or actions for those cards. Remember, practice makes perfect – so shuffle the deck and do the whole exercise again until you make no errors at all.

Extending the memorization

Once you've mastered the 12 court cards, it's showtime! You can now move toward memorizing a complete deck of 52. First, you need to lay the groundwork. Just as you gave a character to each of the court cards, you need to attach a character and a prop, feature or action to the remaining 40 cards in the deck. It sounds laborious, but once it's done, and you use your cast list to memorize cards as they are turned over, you'll have one of the greatest practice tools for your memory at your fingertips.

Coding your cards

If you managed to code the 100 permutations of digits for the Dominic System (see p.92), coding your 40 remaining cards will seem like child's play. Begin by picking out cards that somehow remind you of someone. Perhaps the Ace of Spades is your boss, or a teacher you particularly admired. One of my students uses a whole British pop group – S Club 7 – for the 7 Clubs! I like to use James Bond for the 7 Diamonds – he is agent number 007 and he was the starring character in the movie *Diamonds are Forever*. Once you've been through the remaining 40 cards, finding those with specific character significance, you can code the rest of the cards using a slight adaptation of the Dominic System.

The Dominic System for playing cards

Instead of coding pairs of numbers into pairs of letters that then translate to names, you can use the Dominic System to translate the card value into one letter and then use the initial letter of the suit to give the second letter. For example, the 2 Spades becomes B (2) S (Spades) and the 8 Hearts becomes HH. Unless you've already given specific associations unrelated to the Dominic System, the Ace of any suit takes A and the ten of any suit takes O. Turn through the remaining cards in the deck, working out the letter pairs. Make a list on a sheet of paper (just as you did for the numbers), writing the pairs of letters down the left-hand column. In the next column spell out the character name for each card. For me BS translates to Bram Stoker (the author of *Dracula*), while HH is the wrestler Hulk Hogan, but could equally well be Harry Houdini or Hermann Hesse. Of course, you don't always have to use famous people – if you know someone called Helen Harris, she would work, too. In the next column give each character an action, feature or prop, just as you did on page 94.

Learning your codes

The temptation once you've spent lots of time working out your characters is to set about learning them all straightaway. However, you want to make the codes you've formed stick, so I suggest you adopt a slow, careful learning process that enables you to embed the codes firmly in your mind. Aim to learn ten cards and their characters and actions every day for four days (you already know the 12 court cards). On the fifth day, review the lot – from memory if you can – simply by turning over the cards one at a time and saying to yourself that character's name and prop, feature or action. Include the court cards in your review process, too.

If you like, you can adopt a more formalized approach and review according to the principles of the Rule of Five. Every day learn your ten new characters, but also every day make a review of those characters and any you've learned on previous days (again, including the court cards). In this way, by the time you come to your full review on day five, all the characters should be making their way into your long-term memory. If you can do

EXERCISE 8: A Deck of Cards

It's hugely important for your self-confidence to have lots of small successes that build up to one big success. So, in this exercise, you're going to use the basic system to memorize half a deck of cards. Only once you're confident should you try the full deck.

1 Choose a journey of 26 stages that you're completely familiar with – you don't want to have to work to recall the stages when you're trying to memorize the cards. Once your route is ready, count out 26 of the 52 cards (half the deck) and shuffle them, then place them face down in front of you. Turn over the top card and put it down next to the stack. Connect that card's character and prop, feature or action with the first stop on your journey. When you're ready, turn up the next card, and connect that one to the second stage. Continue turning and mentally placing cards until you've revealed all the cards in the stack.

2 Do a mental review of the journey. The system should allow for good retention, so you shouldn't need to review before you've memorized all 26 cards. As you review, don't refer back to the cards themselves: simply walk through your journey, recalling each card to yourself. Then, for your "official" recall, write down each card in sequence on a sheet of paper. Refer back to the deck of 26 cards to assess how well you did. A score of 10–16 cards in order is very good; 17 or more is excellent. Once you can confidently memorize all 26, try step 3.

3 Now repeat the memorization in steps 1 and 2, but for the whole deck (for this you'll need a route of 52 stages). Once you're confident at that, you can try the advanced system (see opposite).

more reviews than this (perhaps in the morning and evening, each day), all the better. Once you're confident that you know your cards inside out, you're ready to do the exercise on the opposite page. Try it, and be confident with it, before you move on to the advanced system for card memorization described below.

Advanced card memorization

To memorize four digits at a time, you used "complex images" – you combined one character with the prop, feature or action of another (see pp.96–9). You can use the same principle for memorizing cards, and then you need only a 26-stage journey to memorize a whole deck; which means that you can use your 52-stage journey for two decks. This is how it works.

Imagine that the first two cards you turned up in the deck were the 6 Clubs (SC) and the 5 Spades (ES). Let's say that your character for SC is Simon Cowell and his action is pressing the buzzer to register his displeasure at an act on one of his talent shows; while ES gives you the former boxer and famous US talk-show host Ed Sullivan, whose action (naturally) is boxing. At the first stage of the journey, instead of just placing Simon Cowell with his own action (which would represent one card), you'd place Simon Cowell boxing, in this way combining the two cards at one stage. For example, let's say the first stage of your journey is your front door. You might imagine Simon Cowell in boxing gloves pummelling the closed door as if trying to punch his way in. If you pair up the remaining cards in the deck in the same way and place each pair at a stage on your journey, you'll need only 26 stages to memorize all 52 cards.

Playing card games

Once I'd developed my advanced system and become proficient at it so that I could memorize multiple decks of cards with relative ease, I could not only win memory competitions and amaze audiences, I also became a card sharp. For a while I made a living playing the casino game blackjack – I used my powerful memory to gain an edge over the casinos, gambled accordingly, and won good money. Unsurprisingly, I was also eventually banned from casinos on both sides of the Atlantic!

Of course, not everyone will want to hone their card-memorizing skills to become a professional blackjack player, but the system is just as applicable to household games such as whist or bridge. In whist, for example, four players are each dealt 13 cards from a shuffled deck. The object of the game is to win tricks: the highest trump laid in a round wins the trick; or if no player lays a trump, the highest card of the leading suit takes the trick. Let's say you want to memorize the following typical round of cards played in a four-handed game. The four players (column 1, below) lay the following cards (column 2). The third and fourth columns represent my character codes for those cards.

PLAYER 1	3 Clubs	CC	Charlie Chaplin
PLAYER 2	4 Clubs	DC	David Copperfield
PLAYER 3	8 Clubs	HC	Hillary Clinton
PLAYER 4	Ace Clubs	AC	Al Capone

There are a number of ways to approach how you memorize the round, depending on the level of help you feel you need.

First, if you just want to know that these cards have left the deck, try imagining throwing a bucket of water over each of the card characters. I imagine the reaction of each person as they receive a good drenching: Charlie Chaplin's sad face; a rueful expression from David Copperfield; Hillary Clinton shocked and dismayed; and Al Capone giving me an angry, threatening look! Once you have "seen" these actions in your mind, you'll be able to work out whether or not a certain card is still to play, simply by recalling whether or not that character has had a drenching yet.

A more precise method is to use a prepared 26-stage route to memorize the sequence as the cards are played. Using the system of complex images to memorize two cards at a time (one as a character, the other as a prop, feature or action), at the first stage of the journey I picture Charlie Chaplin pulling a rabbit out of a hat (Chaplin is using the action of the magician David Copperfield). At the second stage, I picture Hillary Clinton spraying bullets from a machine gun (Al Capone's action). Once the second round is played, I place that set of four cards at the next two stages of my journey, and so on until all the cards have been played.

Finally, if you feel really confident with the system, you could allocate one journey for each player and memorize which cards have been played by each person. You need four routes of 13 stages. Player 1, to your left, could be a route around a park, player 2's route could be through a shopping mall, and so on. When player 1 lays down the 3 Clubs, you picture Charlie Chaplin at, say, the park gate (the first stage); when player 2 plays the 4 Clubs, you imagine David Copperfield doing magic at the entrance of the shopping mall; and so on.

CHAPTER EIGHTEEN

GETTING UP TO SPEED

The thing about memorizing cards and making it a practical skill to use in card games and in casinos is that you need to be fast. It's not possible for me to teach you speed itself – the more you practise, the faster you'll get – but I can let you in on the secret of how I make my memorizations as fast and efficient as possible.

The simplest way for me to illustrate how I optimize the time I spend is to describe to you exactly how and what I'm thinking as I memorize the first six cards from a shuffled deck.

First, my journey: in my mind's eye I'm standing in the travel agent in Guildford, Surrey. There's no one in the room, but I'm aware of my surroundings – there are holiday advertisements posted on the walls and there's noise from the street outside.

In the real world, I deal two cards in quick succession: the Ace of Diamonds and 7 Clubs. Immediately, I get a vague image of the actor John Cleese, my Ace of Diamonds (the card metamorphosed from Anne Diamond, a newsreader, to Cleese who sat at a desk and said "And now for something completely different"), sitting in a jacuzzi, which is the prop for the 7 Clubs (the 7 Clubs was an immediate association I made for my friend Paul in a jacuzzi). I make a fleeting mental note of my response to this bizarre scene – I think this could be a typical sketch from an episode of *Monty*

INSIDE MY MIND: BREAKING THE SPEED LIMIT

You'll probably find that when you start to get proficient at card memorization, you'll get faster and faster and then hit a barrier – usually at around five or six minutes per deck. How do you break through it? Years ago a competitor told me that she couldn't break her four-minute barrier. I asked her how many mistakes she was making and she told me that every deck she memorized, she recalled perfectly. That was her problem. As strange as it may sound, when I memorize a deck of cards at speed, I will usually make five or six errors. Why don't I strive for perfection? If I don't make any errors, how can I work out at what point I reach my capacity for memorization at the fastest possible speed? By always making one or two errors, I push myself against my boundaries. However, I do need to know what the boundaries are so that, during a competition, I can slow down my time to a pace that I know will mean I won't incur any penalty points.

Perhaps you're thinking that this contradicts my advice to take a zero-failure approach to card memorization. I suppose it does, but when you start out on your memory training, the most important thing to gain is confidence – to believe that you can do it, just as I learned to believe. Once I had that self-belief, I could start to take risks, push the boundaries and stretch my mind and my memory to the very limits of its capabilities – and if that meant making one or two errors along the way, well, I had the confidence to not let that stand in my way on the path to championship success.

Python. In a split second I note that this is a logical fit (Cleese was one of the *Monty Python* team) and move on to the next stage.

I turn another two cards over in quick succession: 6 Spades and Ace of Hearts. Standing at the level crossing I see my wife (the six reminds me of "sexy" and her former name was Smith, which gave me the S for Spades) injecting herself with a drug (my character for the Ace of Hearts is a friend who had something of a misspent youth). I get a momentary sense of shock at this thought – a good sign that I'll recall the scene later.

I turn over two more cards: Jack of Hearts and 10 Spades. Looking through the window of a clothes shop, I see my uncle (who looks like the Jack of Hearts) riding an elephant (irregularly, the 10 Spades is one of two animals in my list of characters – the other being my dog – but you might want to use the Dominic System in which 10 Spades gives you the initials OS). I sense my uncle's embarrassment at sitting on the elephant in a clothes shop.

And, then that's it – first six cards done. How long did it take me? About four seconds!

People assume that I must have a unique talent for visualizing pictures in detail and at great speed. However, as I mentioned earlier, I'm not aware of any great detail in my mind's eye. I don't need a faithful photographic image to recall my card characters. In many ways, it's the emotional responses that I make to the general impression of the scene that are important. When it comes to the recall phase, I do have a sort of distorted picture of the scenes I created during the memorization, but it's the emotional footprint that plays a crucial role in how well I can memorize and recall the sequence of the cards.

Our emotions tend to be instant: they are often knee-jerk reactions to what we see. And they are powerful. It's quicker and more effective to imagine a scene and monitor my emotional response to it, and then afterwards to recapture that emotional response as my memory trigger, than to fill in every last detail of how the image might look in reality.

This may seem to contradict everything I've told you so far about being creative and using your imagination and all your senses. What I've just described is my thought process as I'm memorizing cards at speed. However, when I started out, I liked to exaggerate images and make them as funny, or sad, or even violent as I could to make the information stick. This was certainly useful at first, but in time, with more and more practice and as I've become increasingly proficient, I haven't needed to use precise detail or exaggeration, because creating the journeys, to me, is now more like an alternative real life.

After a while you, too, will rely less on detail, and instead exploit emotional responses. Your journeys will gradually change from being fantastic, slapstick cartoons to more surreal series of episodes with strong emotional connections. But it takes dedication and effort to get to this point – you have to keep practising. Card memorization is one of the best exercises you can give your memory – so the practice itself has enormous value for everyday life. With regular practice (say, once a day for a month), you may even be able to memorize a full deck in close to five minutes. And if you can make it in less than 60 seconds, I could be seeing you at the next World Memory Championships!

CHAPTER NINETEEN

DECODING THE BRAIN: FROM TECHNIQUES TO TECHNOLOGY

I've taught you my main methods for memorization. Now I want to tell you about another way that I train my brain. It all started in 1997 when I was asked to take part in a series of experiments that would measure my brain's activity as I was memorizing. By connecting me to an EEG (electroencephalogram) machine to measure the electrical activity in my brain, the researchers worked at finding out how that activity behaved across the hemispheres, as information passed between them via the corpus callosum, the superhighway that connects the brain's two halves. Researchers looked at both the balance of electrical power between the hemispheres of my brain and the range of brainwave frequencies I produced, according to whether I was memorizing playing cards in their random order or trying to recall them.

Seeing my brainwave activity on a computer screen in real time opened up a whole new world for me – finally, having taught myself techniques that enabled me to undertake great feats of memorization, I had an insight into what was actually going on inside my brain as I was doing this. I had expected that the balance of power would firmly reside in my right hemisphere, but, in fact, the results held a surprise for me. It turned out that each hemisphere produced almost exactly the same overall level of electrical power, or microvolts – neither hemisphere appeared to be more dominant over the other during memorization or recall.

Then, I noticed the frequencies – or speed – at which my brainwaves had been firing. The main brainwave frequencies we produce are:

- Beta waves: These are fast frequencies and represent the brain's normal alert activity. They are vital for taking action, decision making and concentration. Beta frequencies range from 13 to 40 Hertz. With such a broad frequency spectrum, beta waves are often subdivided into high beta and low beta. It's worth mentioning that high beta waves (24 to 40 Hertz) can be associated with stress. In short bursts, frantic brain activity is good for quick thinking and instant reaction, but prolonged high-beta activity is draining and can lead to burn-out.

- Alpha waves: These are slower – they are the "chill out" frequencies that we generate when we're relaxed, and they are the best waves for undertaking creative visualization. They range from 9 to 12 Hertz.

- Theta waves: I think these are the most fascinating brainwave frequencies. Commonly referred to as the brainwaves of the twilight state, theta waves are associated with dreaming and

REM (Rapid Eye Movement) sleep, when many researchers believe our memories are consolidated. During wakefulness, our theta waves promote creative thinking and logical thinking, both of which are important for improving memory. They range from 5 to 8 Hertz.

- Delta waves: These brainwaves are the slowest we experience and are associated with deep sleep and deep physical relaxation. They range in frequency from 1 to 4 Hertz.

As I committed the sequence of 52 cards to memory, I produced the full range of brainwave frequencies from slow delta to fast beta. However, the frequencies were dominated by alpha and theta waves, so I was clearly feeling relaxed – and also creative, which is in line with the process of memorization that I'd devised. During recall, the theta waves became more dominant, indicating that I'd turned up the waves most associated with recall.

I was so impressed and intrigued by what I'd learned that I went out and bought my own equipment. I measure not only my own brainwaves, but those of clients, friends and family, all the time gaining insight into what's going on inside their powerful minds.

Analyzing the results

I've now spent more than a decade analyzing the EEG readings of all sorts of people – from those who claim to have a good memory to those who say they don't; young and old; working and retired. Although everyone's brain is unique, I have noticed that in a relatively small percentage of individuals, who have a

INSIDE MY MIND: TECHNOLOGY AND MY TRAINING

Training for a memory championship is a full-time job for the two or three months before the competition takes place. Along with sorting out my physical well-being (see pp.180–81), I have to get my brain into shape. I take measurements on the EEG (see p.114) and AVS (see pp.119–20) machines that I have at home to make sure the two sides of my brain are communicating well with one another.

The World Memory Championships comprises ten disciplines (see p.97). I practise all these again and again, on a rota, until I'm confident of both my methods and my speed. Typically, I memorize around 600 numbers using three routes of 50 stages, accommodating four digits at each stage, using complex images (see pp.96–9). I have a simple computer program that flashes six binary digits per second on a screen, and I practise memorizing 300 digits, in sequence, in 50 seconds. I also use computer software that recites a 300-digit number at the rate of one digit per second. These are great ways to condition my brain for long periods of intense concentration, while providing essential practice for the Spoken Number discipline. Another computer program randomly selects 300 words from an electronic dictionary, which I try to memorize in 15 minutes, while another generates year dates and random nouns so that I can practise making links between dates and events (during the competition itself, I distil each event description into a key noun). Yet another generates abstract images for me to practise with. Social networking sites, such as Facebook, provide me with practice matching names to faces (I aim for 100 names and faces in 15 minutes).

happy, healthy lifestyle and a noticeably efficient memory, there is a certain pattern of brainwave activity that generally occurs. From concert pianists to CEOs and TV producers to full-time mothers, these individuals have three features in common:

1 Most importantly, they have very good balance in terms of amplitude or power across both hemispheres of their brain.
2 They have mobility through the range of frequencies from beta to delta (that is, they can switch frequencies easily). This is essential for optimizing brain power, in the same way that changing gears is essential for optimizing a car's engine power.
3 They can produce high-powered alpha waves – at 10 Hertz – which shows a good ability to relax and receive information.

Working with the data

So what does knowing all this mean in practice? If you can learn to align your brain to the best frequencies for memorization, you will automatically increase the power of your memory. Two methods by which you can do this using technology are neurofeedback and Audio Visual Stimulation. However, the great news is that I believe (although I haven't made empirical studies of this) that non-machine techniques, such as the memory training ideas in this book, are no less valuable for training your brain to access the best brain frequencies for memorization. In other words, although they might take a bit longer and require more dedication, "manual" techniques can, I believe, be just as effective as the training that I'm doing using a machine. As a matter of interest, though, here's how the machines do the job quickly.

Neurofeedback – look no hands!

Ever wanted to play a computer game using just the power of your brain? It sounds futuristic and even out of this world, doesn't it? But it's perfectly possible. Let's say you're stressed out and producing far too many high-end beta waves (see p.115). You're becoming absent-minded and forgetful. To fix this, you hook yourself up to a neurofeedback system and play a game that requires you to produce slower alpha and theta waves in order to succeed. You might have to move a ball through a maze, but the ball will move only when your beta waves reduce and alpha activity increases, encouraging you to relax your mind. After several sessions of conscious mental relaxation, your brain learns to shift down a gear on its own and your memory starts to perform more efficiently.

Audio Visual Stimulation – Rose-tinted memory specs

Another way to influence your brainwaves is to use Audio Visual Stimulation (AVS). Sitting in a chair, you wear a pair of glasses with in-built light-emitting diodes (LEDs). The lights can be set to flash at a frequency that matches any desired brainwave pattern, which your brain then tunes into. This is called Frequency Following Response. For example, if you want to train your brain to easily access the alpha state, you would then set the program to a 10-Hertz frequency. Then, you close your eyes and sit back and allow your brainwaves to tune in to the flashing lights for about 20 minutes. AVS is an extremely powerful, non-invasive, non-addictive tool for resetting your brain to good working order – I wish every household could have one!

INSIDE MY MIND: REVERSING THE BRAIN DRAIN

I wouldn't be without my EEG and AVS machines. Although it might sound like something from a Gothic horror novel, realigning my brain with these machines is fundamental to my training. When I attempt feats of memorization, I need to be relaxed, but focused. The predominant brainwave frequencies that I need to produce should range between slower theta waves of 5 to 8 Hertz and faster low-end beta waves of 13 to 14 Hertz. If the ratio of beta to theta is less than 3:2, I'm showing signs of stress (this is the number-one common denominator in people I see who say they have a poor memory), in which case I take steps to remove stress from my life (see p.183), including using the AVS.

My AVS unit helps me to fine-tune and balance the electrical activity of my brain. I can set a frequency pattern to either speed up my brain if I'm feeling too dreamy or slow it down if I'm feeling stressed. My brainwaves follow the flashing patterns and learn to produce similar frequencies of their own. As the lights stimulate the billions of neurons in my brain to "dance to the same tune", I get a complete sense of relaxation. Afterwards, I feel centred, the world appears in sharper focus and colours seem brighter. Measurements of my brain activity show that the overall power of my brain in microvolts increases after these sessions. But the most important benefit is that my stress levels fall and I can think more clearly. Interestingly, the degree to which I notice any of these changes depends on how poor my well-being is at that particular time. If I'm already in good shape physically and feeling relaxed, I really don't feel the benefits of the AVS.

CHAPTER TWENTY

THE FIRST WORLD MEMORY CHAMPIONSHIPS

Once I had all my techniques sorted and I started breaking records for memorization, I realized that I needed a new challenge. I had an idea about holding a memory competition that would pit the world's best memorizers against one another. We were already trying to outdo each other for entries in the *Guinness World Records* book every year, so it seemed a natural step to make the competition upfront and official and put us all under one roof to battle for recall supremacy. I knew of a handful of people around the world who were capable of memorizing cards and long sequences of numbers, who I knew would be up to the challenge, but I had one problem. In the interests of fair play, I couldn't devise the competition *and* enter myself – especially if there were even a small chance that I could win.

Before I did any more than muse on the idea, fate was to play its hand. In 1991, I received a letter from chess grandmaster Raymond Keene about an event planned for later the same year. This is what it said:

"Dear Mr O'Brien,

Creighton Carvello suggested that you might be interested in the 1st Memoriad, which we are organizing. I enclose details, and I do hope you will attend. I have, by the way, seen mention of your exploits in the bridge column in The Times, *where I also write the chess column.*

Looking forward to hearing from you,

Best Wishes

Raymond Keene OBE"

I couldn't believe the timing. I felt as though I had spent the previous three years training for such a competition and here it was, handed to me on a plate.

Raymond Keene, with Tony Buzan (who created Mind Maps®; see pp.142–4), had come up with the concept of a Memory Championships and they were now ready to launch this upon the world. The first time I met the two of them, they quizzed me about my techniques and how I'd got involved. When I told them how I performed my memorizations, Tony turned to Raymond with an expression on his face as if to say, "He knows the secrets."

These two co-founders spoke to a number of potential competitors, listened to our recommendations, and made a note of our various memory strengths. Using all this information, they put together the first ever World Memory Championships, which they called the "Memoriad". A mere month later, I and six others (Tony Buzan called us "The Magnificent Seven") competed for the title of first ever World Memory Champion at London's Athenaeum Club.

Dressed in a tuxedo and as prepared as I could be for the one-day event, when I arrived at the club I think I felt most nervous about meeting Creighton Carvello, my inspiration, for the first time. When we did meet (and he was charming), the first thing I noticed about him was that his black shoes were so well polished, I could almost see my reflection in them. If his performance was going to be as polished as his shoes, I stood no hope at all!

The competition between us all was fierce, but with grave determination I clinched the title in the last discipline – memorizing at speed a single deck of shuffled cards. In what seemed a fitting end to three years of hard brain training, I beat Creighton Carvello's record for a single deck by a satisfying 30 seconds: I did it in 2 minutes 29 seconds, with no errors.

Two decades of championships later, the rules and individual disciplines have been honed and refined to accommodate the suggestions of first-class memorizers from all over the world. You've already learned how to do most of the disciplines in the process of learning how to supercharge your memory power, notably the rounds relating to numbers and playing cards, but also by extension the random words round – all of which you could attempt with the techniques I've taught you so far. It's really heartwarming to me that I can claim responsibility for suggesting two of the other events in the competition: 15-minute memorization of abstract images (more of these later), and the discipline that I want to teach you next, the 30-minute memorization of random binary digits, which I believe to be a supreme training routine for your brain.

CHAPTER TWENTY-ONE

CHAMPIONSHIP PRACTICE: BINARY DIGITS

The first ever World Memory Championships was enormously well received, by both the competitors and the media. For the following year, we knew that the competition had to be bigger and better and stretch the memorizers even further. I suggested to the organizers that memorizing binary digits would be a great test of an individual's memory power and ingenuity. Binary digits also make a great exercise for anyone who wants to learn to boost their memory power.

Binary code is the language by which all computers work – it represents the two positions in which a switch can operate: on (1) or off (0). So, when you see a binary sequence, it's merely a series of ones and zeroes. Below is a row of 30 ones and zeroes in a random order. How would you go about memorizing them in their correct sequence?

1 1 0 0 1 1 0 0 1 0 1 0 0 1 1 0 1 0 1 1 1 1 1 1 0 0 1 1 0 1

You can see why I thought a binaries round would be a great test of mental agility! This no doubt seems a tough challenge – although, of course, 30 digits wasn't nearly enough to tax the brains of the greatest memorizers in the world. For this discipline, competitors at the World Memory Championships are presented with at least 100 rows of 30 binary numbers and they have just half an hour to commit them all, in sequence, to memory.

In 1997, I managed to memorize 2,385 binary numbers in 30 minutes. At the time I set a new world record, but since then others have done better. How is this possible? Well, like everything to do with feats of memorization, you need a system. In fact, once you've mastered the Dominic System (see pp.90–95), memorizing binary numbers is relatively straightforward.

My solution for cracking binaries was to create a code that turned them into numbers I could work with. I worked out all the possible groups of three binaries there could be and then gave each group of three a number code. So:

000 = 0	110 = 4
001 = 1	100 = 5
011 = 2	010 = 6
111 = 3	101 = 7

My system is simple – the first four combinations are represented by their sum and the last four simply continue the sequence of decimal numbers in a way that seems logical to me. To memorize a binary number, all you have to do is to memorize the codes, work out how they apply to the binary number and apply the

Dominic System to turn the "proper" numbers into characters, which you place along a journey. In the Championships event, competitors are permitted to write the codes for the groups of three (or whatever system they're using) across the top of the binary digits.

You might think that learning how to memorize binaries has no benefit to you at all. However, if you want to attain a perfect memory, memorizing binary sequences is a fantastic practice exercise, because it combines all the elements that make up the best methods of memorization. So, please bear with me.

Here's another sequence of 24 binary digits. This time I have converted them into their code numbers (in brackets):

1 1 0 (4)
0 1 1 (2)
0 0 1 (1)
0 1 0 (6)
1 0 1 (7)
1 0 1 (7)
0 1 1 (2)
0 1 0 (6)

Once I've made the conversion, I pair the numbers, so that I get:

42 16 77 and 26.

And then to each of these I apply a character, using the Dominic System, which gives me:

David Beckham, Arnold Schwarzenegger, Ga Ga (Lady) and Bart Simpson. (You should use your own characters if you can, as they will be more memorable to you.)

When you position these characters along the journey, you use complex images (see pp.96–9), so that the first character in a pair becomes a surrogate for the action of the character that represents the second pair of numbers. So in fact, to memorize those 24 binary digits, I need only two stages of my chosen journey.

STAGE 1   I picture the English footballer David Beckham (42) weight-lifting. Beckham is using the action I associate with Arnold Schwarzenegger (16).

STAGE 2   I imagine the singer Lady Gaga (77) acting like Bart Simpson (26) and shouting "Eat my shorts!"

This sounds complicated and you may think that following so many processes just to memorize a series of ones and zeroes seems laborious and long-winded. However, your brain is an amazing machine – its processing speed is far faster than any computer. Think of the pianist who can convert notes to music in tenths of a second (a skilled pianist can read up to 20 notes in a second) so that he plays his pieces flawlessly. Even as you read this sentence your brain is converting letters into sounds and giving them meaning without your consciousness giving you time to dwell on the process at all. It's all about practice, and when you know how to do it, and you work at getting better, like anything it can become second nature to you. Now try the exercise on the following page.

EXERCISE 9: Binary Bonanza

OK – so now it's your turn. If your brain can cope with the various levels of function required to get this right, you're well on the way to your amazing memory.

1 Using the codes on page 125, convert the following 30 binary digits into workable numbers. Note down the codes for each set of three digits on a sheet of paper.

  0 1 1 0 1 0 1 1 1 1 0 0 1 0 1 0 0 0 0 0 1 1 0 1 1 1 0 0 1 1

2 You have just 1 minute for the rest of the memorization element of this exercise (converting the codes to letters, then characters and placing these on a journey). Set a timer and then begin your memorization. When you've finished, write down on a sheet of paper the sequence of binaries (go straight to the binaries – don't write down the codes). Look back at the list to check how you did. A score of 18–24 binary digits is good; 25–30 is excellent.

3 Once you've completed this exercise successfully and confidently, ask a friend or family member to write you another list of 30 binary digits; or, using your computer, shut your eyes and just allow your fingers to type zeroes and ones randomly until you have a new sequence you can use for practice. This time, give yourself a minute and a half, but try to incorporate the conversion to workable numbers into your time window – go from binary to memorization against the clock, as in the real World Memory Championships.

CHAPTER TWENTY-TWO

CHAMPIONSHIP PRACTICE: NAMES AND FACES

Once I'd won the first World Memory Championships (or The Memoriad, as it was known then) in 1991, I was thrust into the limelight, appearing in the news media across the world. Before too long I had taken on a manager and was soon appearing on TV on chat shows and game shows, demonstrating card memorization and showing the world that I could memorize the names and faces of entire audiences.

It's a funny thing being known for your amazing memory – it adds a certain pressure to perform at all times. If I'm at a function or if I'm teaching a room full of people how to improve their memory, it would be incongruous (and downright embarrassing!) to call someone by the wrong name. Being able to recall someone's name is an important social skill for any of us – and for me it's about proving that I can do what I say I can do, every time I meet a new face. It's also one of the heats in the World Memory Championships, and like binary digits it makes a great practice exercise for training your memory.

At the World Memory Championships, competitors are presented with photographs of 100 named faces and given just 15 minutes to memorize the faces and their corresponding first names and surnames. The photographs are then presented again in a fresh, random order and competitors have to match them up correctly. Let me tell you, they aren't always easy names! Competitors come from all over the world, so it's only fair that the names do, too – and we have to spell every single one correctly, or lose points. You can understand how mastering this stands me in good stead when I'm in a live situation with real people in front of me.

To give you a flavour of what competitors face, here are a few names taken from actual World Memory Championships sessions: Detlef Sokolowski, Hlelile Esposito, Ahlf Vogel, Gad Hotchkiss, Xiulan Majewski. So you see, it's quite a feat of memorization to get them all right. At the time of writing, the world record holder is Boris Konrad from Germany, who memorized 97 names and faces correctly in the 15 minutes.

So how is it done? And does it make a good exercise for your memory? World Memory Championships competitors each have their own variations on several methods to memorize names and faces, but all of them follow the same principles, combining association, location and imagination.

Name associations

In order to memorize names to go with faces, names, like numbers, need to be translated into images. Let's say you're introduced to a man called Rupert Watts. For whatever reason, this man reminds you of your dentist – stick with this instant association and imagine the man in a dentist's white coat. What connections do you make for the name Rupert? Perhaps you think of someone famous: Rupert Everett the actor, or Rupert Murdoch the media tycoon? For me, Rupert gives "Rupert Bear", the children's comic-strip character. I picture a scene at my dentist's surgery where Rupert, dressed in white, is carrying a dental drill. "Watts" I associate with electricity, so I imagine Rupert Bear changing a light bulb in the surgery. The next time I meet this person, he'll remind me again of my dentist and the chain of associations will fast-forward his name to me.

Feature links

What happens if the person you meet doesn't immediately remind you of someone? In these cases, I try to find a link between some physical feature in that person and their name. For example, I meet a woman called Tina who is not very tall – tiny Tina. Her surname is Bellingham, so I imagine tiny Tina ringing a bell coated with a slice of ham (BELL/rING/HAM).

The truth is, of course, that many names don't provide such a convenient link with a feature, but usually something is there. Rupert Watts might have a "pert" nose, or someone called Oliver Childs might have olive-shaped eyes or olive-coloured skin. It doesn't usually matter if the link is tenuous – it just has to be a little visual hook that triggers an association to reveal the name.

Beam me up Scotty

It's not always a visual feature (a likeness or physical characteristic) that triggers the context of a name memorization. Sometimes the name itself holds the key. For example, if someone tells me their surname is Holmes, I can transport that person to 221b Baker Street in London, home of the fictional sleuth Sherlock Holmes. I kit out the person's face with as many Sherlock Holmes connections as I can think of. I might imagine him (or her) wearing the deerstalker hat and smoking a pipe. Then, I have to plant the person's first name in the scene. If it's a man and he's called Peter, I imagine my father (also Peter) knocking on the door at 221b Baker Street, which Sherlock Holmes then opens. If it's a woman called Andrea, I imagine an android serving tea in Holmes's study.

"Hello, my name's Arthur Stanislofsachinkolovspedeten"

We live in a diverse, multicultural society and as we travel more and meet interesting people from many different cultures, names and, in particular, surnames, can present quite a challenge for even a seasoned memorizer like me. To make these stick, I have to break down the names into more manageable chunks.

So, for example, a surname such as Sokolowski becomes an image of a "sock on a low ski". Keeping with the sock theme, for Esposito, I would imagine a sock with a hole to "expose a toe". Have a go at thinking up associations to help you remember "Arthur Stanislofsachinkolovspedeten" – what weird and wonderful ideas can you come up with? Your brain, like mine, loves finding patterns and making links, so there's always a way to make connections to help your memorization. (Test your associations tomorrow by writing the name down on a piece of paper and then looking back to see how close you are – did you get the spelling right?)

How to memorize a room full of people

So, if that's how it's done when I'm introduced to one person at random, or when I compete in championships, how do I show off my skills with a room full of people? I regularly give presentations, and my *pièce de résistance* is to memorize the names of every person in the room. If I have around 50 people in attendance, that's pretty simple – it's two fewer than a deck of cards! This time, instead of placing card characters along a journey, I put real people in their imagined guises at each stage. Remember my memory journey bank? I have several memory journeys of 50 stages that I save especially for memorizing names – I can link the journeys together, as I do with long card sequences, if I need to.

This is how it works. The first person in the room tells me their name. Immediately, I fix him or her to the first stage of my journey. Let's say that's the car park at my golf club. I imagine that I'm standing with that person in the car park. As I think about this image, I repeat the name out loud and look carefully at the person's face. What jumps out at me? Do they have a pointed nose? Curly hair? A scar on their brow or a mole on their upper lip? Does he or she remind me of someone I know, or of someone famous? Sometimes all I need is a small idiosyncrasy or mannerism to hook on to. Once I've fixed the image and made the associations with the name, I move on to the next stage in my journey and the next person in the room. I keep going until I've memorized every person there and their name.

The system works whether people are seated in an auditorium or moving around, because I can "place" the face at the right stage of the journey as soon as I see it again, even if the person is not actually

EXERCISE 10 (PART 1): Don't I Know You From Somewhere?

There's no substitute for being in a room full of people and having to memorize all their names, but this exercise is a good second best, and it's exactly how it works in the World Memory Championships, so it provides great practice.

Study the following ten faces. Use your powerful imagination to make a connection between each name and face, using the techniques outlined in this chapter. (You can use a journey if it helps you, but I won't ask you to repeat them in the right order, so you don't necessarily need one.)

You have 5 minutes to complete the memorization (and as long as you like to attempt the recall). When your 5 minutes are up, turn the page, where you'll find the same faces in a different order. Can you recall the first name and surname that goes with each of those faces?

BRIAN
MCGRATH

JACQUELINE
DACEY

BEN
COBURN

CHARLIE
KNOTT

JOSEPH
FLUTE

JUDY
BARRATT

ABDULLAH
SINGH

MERIEL
DALBY

TED
DOYLE

EMMA
STEVENS

sitting in the same location as when I memorized them. However, I don't usually do an entire auditorium or room in one go. We all have a "forgetting threshold", after which memorizations begin to be a bit hazy. The threshold may vary according to what kind of memorization you're doing – mine is pretty high for numbers (around 200 numbers) and cards (around 100 cards), but I know from experience that my threshold for names and faces is 15. After the 15th name and face I've memorized, I need to do a review of my journey so far (see pp.75–80), retracing my steps and the associations in my head, to be sure that I've made strong connections. Occasionally, I may have to ask someone to repeat their name because the link I made initially wasn't strong enough – I don't like doing this, but it does sometimes happen. Only once I've made my review can I feel confident about moving on to the next 15 names and the faces that go with them. Bear in mind that your own forgetting threshold might be greater or smaller than 15. It's important that you work out – by trial and error – where this is and space your reviews appropriately.

Practice makes perfect

Social networking websites are marvellous for providing names and faces to test your skills of memorization. If you want to get really good at this – and practising really is the only way to do it – log onto MySpace or Facebook and pick some names and faces at random to practise making the connections. You'll soon develop your own instincts for forging links. For now, try the exercise opposite (part 2 – the jumbled-up faces – appears on the following page).

EXERCISE 10 (PART 2): Don't I Know You From Somewhere?

Here are the same ten faces you memorized on page 134, but this time jumbled up. Can you remember their names? There are 20 names in all, ten first names and ten surnames. For each name you get right, award yourself one mark (total: 20 possible marks). A score of 12–15 is good; 16 or more is excellent.

CHAPTER TWENTY-THREE

CHAMPIONSHIP PRACTICE: ABSTRACT IMAGES

In 2006, I introduced a new discipline to the World Memory Championships: Abstract Images. It's a perfect test of someone's memory. Performing well requires no language skills, maths ability, or verbal reasoning – it's a memory "leveller", if you like, a pure test of memory agility, using the power of the imagination. Given 15 minutes, competitors must memorize as many black-and-white abstract shapes, presented in rows of five, as possible, in sequence. Once the 15 minutes are up, they are given a sheet showing the same images, but in a new order. They have to number the images on this second sheet to reflect the original position of each image.

I approach the challenge by looking at the images one by one and finding the first and fastest visual associations I can. Take a look at the following first row of five images. What do you "see"?

1   2   3   4   5

This is how they look to me:

1 A goat's head
2 A garden gnome
3 An oversized jockey riding a squirrel
4 A rabbit
5 A bat in flight

Once I have my associations I use them to create a story that helps me to memorize the correct order of the images. For example, I imagine a goat pecking at a garden gnome and, as he does so, a racing squirrel rushes by. The squirrel jumps over the rabbit, which is eating a bat.

I then place this mini-story at the first stage of the journey I reserve for abstract images (the first stage of my images journey is my back garden) to indicate that these were the images in the first row of five. Then, I memorize the next row of five images in exactly the same way, and place it in my predetermined journey at the second stage – around my garden shed. The journey preserves the order of the rows, while each story I create preserves the order of the images within each row. Here's a sample second row (this time I haven't numbered the images – this is because they aren't numbered in the Championships round, so it's more true to life):

What objects do the images conjure up in your mind's eye?

From left to right I see a funny little alien, a poodle looking up, someone praying, a big-nosed man in a strange hat, and a deer with short antlers. So, I imagine an alien opening the door to my garden shed, which is guarded by a poodle. Inside I see a man praying for mercy. He's being held captive by the guy in a hat. Nailed up on the shed wall is the head of a deer with short antlers.

Here are the same two rows of images, but in a different order:

By replaying the scene from my back garden I know that the original order for the images in the row above is: 4, 3, 2, 5, 1.

Cover the opposite page. Can you recall the original order for the images from row two?

In these examples, I've given you my associations, but of course different associations may have seemed more obvious to you. Each time the challenge is to find an association as quickly as possible and to work each one quickly into a memorable story. This provides a great way to hone your imagination and association skills. Try the exercise on the following page for yourself.

EXERCISE 11: Shape Shifting

Have a go at memorizing the three rows of abstract images in step 1, below. You have 5 minutes (set a timer to alert you when the time is up). Then, cover step 1 and try to restore the jumbled-up images in step 2 to their original order. Recalling two complete rows in the correct order is good; all three is excellent.

1 MEMORIZE THE IMAGES

2 REORDER THE IMAGES

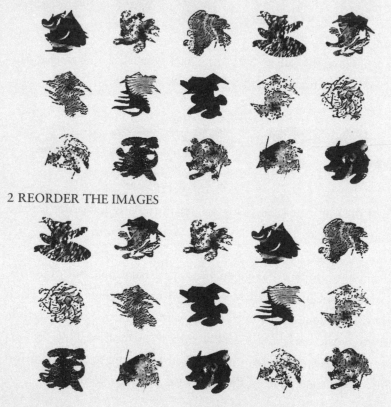

CHAPTER TWENTY-FOUR

THE MEMORY CHAMPION'S LIFE: MAKING SPEECHES

As well as being expected to display impeccable memorization of every new person I met, I soon started to appear on TV shows to demonstrate my memory skills. Imagine: here I was, a man who as a kid had had no self-esteem at all. Now, all of a sudden, I had to learn how to present myself intelligently, express my thoughts clearly and overcome shyness in front of potentially millions of people at any one time. Thank goodness that proving to myself I had good brain power had done wonders for my confidence!

Even so, public speaking certainly wasn't my thing, and apparently I was in good company. The 19th-century American author Mark Twain (of *Huckleberry Finn* fame) was the guest speaker at a dinner with all the great leaders of the American Civil War. After they had made their long, heavy-going speeches, Twain stood up nervously to say, "Caesar and Hannibal are dead, Wellington has gone to a better world and Napoleon is under the sod. And, to be honest, I don't feel too good myself" – and promptly sat down. Things don't seem to have changed with time, either: in the USA a survey has claimed that many people fear making a speech in front of others more than they fear death!

Naturally, the greatest cause for speech anxiety is that your mind will go blank and at best you might start to babble something vaguely coherent, while at worst no sound comes out at all. In which case, read from notes, right? However, think about the most impressive speeches you've heard. Are they read by someone whose eyes look down and whose hands turn over pages? Probably not. The most engaging, inspiring speeches are those given by a speaker who makes eye-contact with the audience, smiles at them and talks as if it all comes naturally. Memorize your speech and people will love to listen. And that's exactly what I had to master when I started giving talks, both on and off camera.

Be prepared!

A poorly prepared speech gets you off on the wrong footing. One of the best pieces of advice I've ever been given about delivering a good speech is, "Say what you are going to say, say it, then say what you just said." If you plan your speech before you write it, you can make sure that you edit out any information that's irrelevant or boring and structure the speech coherently, before you actually start writing the speech itself.

One of the best methods of preparation is a Mind Map®. Devised by Tony Buzan, co-founder of the World Memory Championships, Mind Maps provide a visual means by which to organize information around a central topic. In the centre of the "map" is the topic itself (the topic of your speech, in this case) then, as ideas and thoughts come to you, branches lead out from

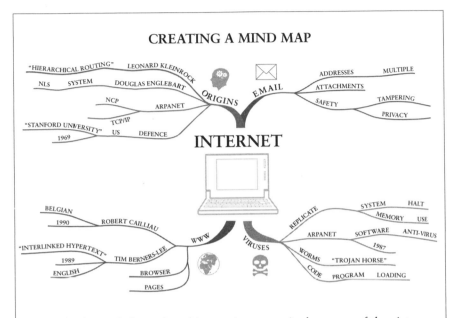

CREATING A MIND MAP

In a Mind Map® the main subject topic appears in the centre of the picture, and key ideas and pieces of information radiate outward. The picture enables you to organize information logically, so that you can construct a coherent speech, while also creating a visual memory trigger.

the centre, breaking down until you have a complete picture that shows everything you want to say. The aim is that this overview shows you where the links are between the elements of your topic, giving you a natural, coherent organization.

Let's say your speech is about the Internet. You write the word "Internet" in a circle in the middle of a sheet of paper, or perhaps you draw a computer. To make your Mind Map especially effective, you use a different colour for each main branch that leads from that central image – it's much easier to navigate around your map if it's colour-coded, and much easier to recall (think about how difficult it would be to navigate the map of a metro system if the different lines weren't defined by colour). Perhaps you could use brown for email, red for viruses, green for the World Wide Web, yellow for the origins of the Internet, and so on. From each of these main branches, sub-topics (sub-branches) will occur to you. You can use a combination of icons and single-word descriptions to organize the sub-topics along their appropriate main branches.

The great thing about this tool is that it allows your brain to work randomly and creatively in planning your speeches, because it is not confined to the restrictions of linear preparation. You can attach topics and sub-topics as they occur to you without having to finish one before moving on to another. Once you've finished, with all your topics in full view, you can use your judgment about which branch you talk about first, and how to continue, until you've covered all the branches. I number the branches and sub-branches to create the most natural, logical order of presentation.

Once you've decided how to organize your speech, make a numbered list of the main points in order, using the numbers on your Mind Map as a guide. For a short speech I usually get this down to five bullet points (each bullet represents about two to five minutes of talking time) – although a long talk will probably have up to 20. Once you've got your bullet points, you just need to memorize them using the Journey Method.

Applying a journey to your speech

The Journey Method provides you with the perfect memory aid to keep you on track during your speech, because you imagine yourself moving from point to point through the journey. If someone interrupts you with a question, you can immediately take yourself back to the position in the journey at which you were interrupted and pick up from where you left off.

So, once you have your bullet points, you need to give each one a visual representation that you can place at each stop on your chosen journey (I have several favourite speech journeys I store in my memory journey bank). I try to keep my visual cues as simple as possible, but when you first start out, you may need to replay a little scene in your mind at each stop to remember certain things that you want to say – such as a relevant date.

In the speech about the Internet, you might start with information about its origins. The Internet was believed to have been born out of systems used for US defence. If my journey begins at my front door, I visualize this as Barack Obama pushing a big red panic button, which takes the place of the doorbell. This is enough to trigger the research I've done about the particular defence strategy that the Internet was used for. But how can I be sure to memorize 1969, the year that it all happened?

Using the Dominic System, 1969 gives me AN and SN, which I convert to the Swedish scientist Alfred Nobel (of Nobel Prize fame) and the actor Sam Neill. I imagine Alfred Nobel on a dinosaur (my prop for Sam Neill, who starred in *Jurassic Park*) coming to the door to give Barack Obama a prize. These images are enough to let me talk for a few minutes on the origins of the Internet. Once I've begun the speech, the visual memory of the Mind Map comes back to fill in some blanks. In the meantime, I mentally move to the next stop on my journey and the next point.

Applying the Link Method

I have many clients, ranging from TV personalities to businessmen and -women, who come to me for regular help with memorization techniques. One such client is a top British comedian. Years ago, he got into the habit of using an autocue to help him recall the gags in his act. The rolling script in front of him gave him two- or three-word descriptions of each gag or mini-routine. As he told one gag, he could see the cue words for the following gag come up on the autocue. Initially, the system worked well – his cue words for each gag were enough to help him stick to the sequence of jokes without it looking as though he were reading from the autocue. However, gradually his confidence in his own memory slipped away and he began to use more and more words on the autocue. Instead of just one or two words per gag, he was using one or two cue words for *each element* of a gag, which meant that the overall routine looked less and less natural. The autocue was acting as a substitute for his working memory. When the severe doubts crept in, he called me for help.

I introduced him to the Journey Method – and he was a natural. A comedian with a highly creative imagination, he has no trouble using a mental journey to separate out the elements of each anecdote or joke and post one element at a time as a coded key image at the relevant stage of a route. He could use as many cues as he wanted per gag, because they were all in his head, so it never appeared to the audience as though the routine was scripted.

However, the Journey Method alone didn't help him go from one gag to the next, and that's why he incorporated the Link Method (see pp.37–42), too: as he gets to the end of one joke (the end of

EXERCISE 12: Stand-up Comedian

How many times have you heard a comedian rattle off a series of short gags, promised yourself you'll remember them to tell your friends, but then completely forgotten them? The Journey Method can change that for ever. Create an associated image for each of the following ten jokes, then link that image to stages on a ten-stop journey. Test the effectiveness of your links by doing a little stand-up show for a willing friend! Repeating five or six jokes in a row from memory is good; seven or more is excellent.

1   A little girl said to her dad that she'd like a magic wand for Christmas, and then added, "And don't forget to put the batteries in!"
2   The lottery: A tax on people who are bad at maths!
3   Suburbia: Where they tear out the trees and name the streets after them!
4   A Buddhist monk walked up to a hot-dog stand and said, "Make me one with everything!"
5   Money talks. Mine generally says "Bye!"
6   Why was Santa's little helper depressed? Because he had low elf-esteem.
7   If at first you don't succeed, skydiving isn't for you.
8   Animal testing is a terrible idea – they get all nervous and give you the wrong answers!
9   If you told a cow a really funny joke, could she laugh so much that milk came out of her nose?
10 You know, when you've seen one shopping centre, you've seen a mall!

his journey), he sees a key image of the next gag cued up in his imagination and waiting for him. This acts as a memory trigger. For example, let's say the story he is telling is set on a riverboat and the gag that follows involves his uncle. As he delivers the punchline about the riverboat, he then sees in his mind's eye his uncle standing on the riverbank in a familiar pose. The key image of his uncle acts as a memory prompt or mental cue to allow him to move confidently on to the next joke in his repertoire (and that is enough to start him off on his next journey).

This combination of using a familiar route to memorize the elements of a funny story or gag and the Link Method to connect the stories or gags together guarantees him a completely polished and convincing performance.

Of course, working in this way is not just for stand-up routines – it can also work for long speeches or talks. For example, if you're conducting a training session for a group of new recruits in your field of work, you'll have several topics to cover over the course of, say, a morning. The company's structure, the ethos of the working environment, the main duties of the job, the telephone systems, and so on, are all aspects of a new job you may have to impart. In the same way that a comedian creates a journey for a particular gag and uses a link to go from one gag to the next, you would use one journey per topic and then use the Link Method to conjure up a visual symbol of the following topic at the end of each journey. The possibilities for the system are endless.

CHAPTER TWENTY-FIVE

THE MEMORY CHAMPION'S LIFE: HOW TO BE A FACT FACTORY

For the summer of 1993, I became Radio 2's "Memory Man", touring with the station up and down the UK, so that the public could test my knowledge of number-one hits spanning the previous 40 years. Once a week, the DJ asked a member of the roadshow audience to shout out their date of birth. I then had to tell the audience member the title of the UK's number one single on that date, who the singer or artist was, how many weeks the song had remained at number one, and which record label it was issued on.

For example, if someone shouted out that their date of birth was February 23, 1956, I could tell them that the number-one single on that date was "Memories are Made of This" sung by Dean Martin. It was at number one for four weeks and released on the Capitol label.

How did I do it? To memorize the number ones, I gave each of the 40 years of hits its own journey, each month in that year an area on the route and each number-one single a specific stage within that area – usually there were around 20 number ones each year, so the total requirement was 40 journeys of around 20 stages (subdivided into month areas). At each stage, I placed a coded scene for the date that week's chart was released, the single's title, the artist, the weeks at number one and the record label.

So, for the Dean Martin single, the process went like this. The person was born in 1956, so I immediately go to my route for that year, which is the upstairs of my brother-in-law's house. I need the month February, and I know that that is represented by the corridor. So I have my position for the year and month. The date I've been given is February 23, which I know fell in the chart week that began on February 21. February 21 is represented by the visual clue of my friend Julia holding a key (21 is the "key to the door" in the rhyme and Julia always used to carry a huge bunch of keys) and she's standing by the door to the linen cupboard on the corridor. Inside the cupboard I see a large, pulsating brain – this is my trigger for "**Memories** are Made of This". I know what Dean Martin looks like, so he's there, too, and he's wearing a white **cap** (which gives me **Capi**tol Records). However, he's not just standing by the cupboard, he's in a sailboat – the sail is the number–shape (see p.83) for 4 – four weeks at number one. (If there's more than one number one in a month, the different singles appear in different places at the one location, but as it happens, Dean Martin held his position at the top spot throughout February 1956.)

Mnemonic devices

Memorizing facts and figures using the Dominic System and the Journey Method will make you a formidable opponent in a general-knowledge quiz (I've memorized all the Trivial Pursuit

EXERCISE 13: Factoid Fun

Here is a selection of ten UK number-one hits from the 1980s. Try to memorize the year that each song became number one. This is a lot easier than it sounds. Use the Dominic System to translate the years into characters, which you can then use to form associations with the song titles. For example, for me, 88 (HH) becomes the wrestler Hulk Hogan. To link Hulk to the hit single, I picture him wrestling with a monkey and George Michael is the referee.

You have 10 minutes to commit the following to memory. Once you've finished, from memory write down the tracks and their years and artists. Score a maximum of three points for each song (one point each for the year, title and artist). A score of 18–24 is good; 25 or more is excellent.

1980 "Rock with You" *Michael Jackson*
1981 "Physical" *Olivia Newton-John*
1982 "Eye of the Tiger" *Survivor*
1983 "Beat It" *Michael Jackson*
1984 "Jump" *Van Halen*
1985 "Heaven" *Bryan Adams*
1986 "Sledgehammer" *Peter Gabriel*
1987 "Open Your Heart" *Madonna*
1988 "Monkey" *George Michael*
1989 "Eternal Flame" *The Bangles*

answers, too!), but even simple mnemonic devices have a firm place in our repertoire of memory techniques.

A word derived from the name Mnemosyne, the Greek goddess of memory, a *mnemonic* is any device that helps us to memorize a piece or pieces of information. The Journey Method, number–shapes and number–rhymes, and all the tricks for memorizing you've learned so far, are all systems of mnemonics. These help us to translate information into meaningful symbols, pictures, words and phrases so that our minds can more easily store them (in turn making them easier to recapture). Some of the simplest mnemonic systems are the most useful for storing facts or pieces of trivia. Below are some of my favourites.

Acronyms and extended acronyms

LOL, BTW, KIT – we live in a world where texting, "tweeting" and instant messaging encourages us to make frequent shorthand communications. Many of us use initial letters as shorthand in written – or spoken – sentences on a daily basis. (Those few mean "laugh out loud", "by the way" and "keep in touch".) Even if you don't text, you probably talk in shorthand about the BBC or CBS, ADHD and PMS. Acronyms are even easier, because they use the initial letters of the words you want to memorize to form another recognizable word. For example, if you were learning about atoms, you would learn that they are made up of protons, electrons and neutrons – PEN.

Extended acronyms, on the other hand, take the letter of each word to make a memorable sentence. For example, to memorize the seven continents (Europe, Asia, Africa, Australia, Antarctica,

North America, South America), think of the phrase "Eat An Apple As A Nice Snack".

Here's a phrase I devised to memorize the seven deadly sins (Anger, Pride, Covetousness, Lust, Sloth, Envy and Greed): "A Politically Correct Liberal Seldom Enters Government!"

Extended acronyms are put to good use by medical students, who have to remember complicated anatomical terms. To remember the eight small bones in the wrist: Navicular, Lunate, Triquetral, Pisiform, Multangular (greater), Multangular (lesser), Capitate and Hamate: "Never Lower Tilly's Pants, Mother Might Come Home!"

How would you go about using an extended acronym to memorize the nine muses? (Incidentally, they were the daughters of Mnemosyne and the king of the gods, Zeus.) They are:

CALLIOPE • CLIO • ERATO • THALIA • EUTERPE • MELPOMENE • TERPSICHORE • POLYHYMNIA • URANIA

You might think of "Count Clambering Elephants Thundering Eastward, Mighty Trunks Pointing Up", or you might bend the rules a bit and make it a more fluid sentence using a few more of the letters or sounds: "Call Clio ET. You (Eu) Twerp Mel, Turps isn't Polyurethane!" The benefit of this second version is that it gives you more of the sounds from the names, which might help your recall – especially with unfamiliar names or terms.

I like to think of mnemonic devices such as acronyms as my "pocket" memory techniques – the easy memory systems that I keep at hand to make it easier to lodge facts as I pick them up.

CHAPTER TWENTY-SIX

USING THE TOOLS: STUDY AND LEARNING

We gather information from all sorts of places. If you're a student, you might be taught in a classroom by a teacher, or on your own from a book, an educational film or the Internet. If you're a businessman or -woman, or even a teacher yourself, you'll have reports, training documents, journals and so on to read and understand. However you've received it, information has to find its way into your long-term storage, so that you can retrieve it whenever you need to – whether that's in an exam, in a meeting, or to teach to others.

The place where most of us did most of our formal learning is school. Estimates vary as to how much of the information we are taught at school we actually remember for any length of time. According to research by The William Glasser Institute, in California, we retain only ten percent of the information we absorb from reading, while we retain approximately half of the information we see and hear, and personal experience gives us around 80 percent retention. The research also shows that if we actively teach something, we retain around 95 percent of the information we pass on to others.

So, what does this tell us? First, and most importantly, it tells us that when we engage actively in a "live" situation, we are more likely to retain information. Second, it shows us that personal experience (which involves action and the senses) is far more likely to lead to long-term storage and retrieval than detached learning methods, such as reading. When we teach information, not only do we have to repeat it, we also have to have understood it, which reinforces the initial learning, embedding it in the brain.

For me, there are four key skills when it comes to success in learning, no matter what the method:

- Absorbing knowledge effectively
- Note-taking
- Memorizing
- Reviewing

Reading efficiently and effectively

The truth is that much of the information we need to learn, to pass exams or do our job, comes from reading – whether you're trying to learn a topic at college or learn figures to present at a team meeting. If you want to maximize the efficiency of learning from the printed word, you might think that reading more slowly and deliberately, trying to retain every detail, is the way forward. However, studies show that reading more quickly, as long as you do this properly, is more likely to get the information to stick. The best method is to use a pointer that you can run along the words as you read them. A pen or even your index finger will do. Research indicates that pointing to each word as you read it significantly increases concentration levels during reading, and also – perhaps surprisingly – the speed at which you read.

Making notes on the key points

I recommend that you read for 20 minutes at a time, before finding a suitable stopping point so that you can make notes. You need to identify the key points in the text you've read and note them down on a sheet of paper. A Mind Map® is the perfect visual store for information we derive from print. See pages 142–4 on how to create one for your topic. Ideally, you should be able to distil your reading from the memory of what you've just read – without looking back, which will slow down the note-taking (but there's no harm in looking back if you need to).

Memorizing the key points

Once you have your key points, you can organize the information and code it into something you can memorize. Do this in exactly the same way that I taught you to memorize speeches (see pp.144–5). On your Mind Map, number the main points in your topic, write these main points in a list and then turn each into a visual key. Place each visual key along a journey of the appropriate number of stages and – hey presto! – you've memorized the important elements of the information you've just read.

Memorizing dates

Whether you're studying history or literature, economics or geography, being able to memorize dates effectively is essential. Let's say you're studying history, and you need to commit to memory the key dates in the American War of Independence. The war began on April 19, 1775; the first major battle between British and American troops, the Battle of Bunker Hill, took place on June 17, 1775; the American Navy was established to fight the British on November 28, 1775; on January 9, 1776, Thomas Paine's *Common Sense* pamphlet was published; then July 4, 1776, finally saw the American Declaration of Independence.

To memorize these dates and events, you'd use a prearranged journey – perhaps a journey around your school would work well – and then code each event and date into a colourful scene for each stop. So, let's say that the first stop is the school gates. The information you need to place there is April 19, 1775, the start of the War. I imagine a starting pistol being fired at the school gates and it's pouring with rain (April showers). I imagine my friend Anne (19 = AN, which gives me the sound trigger for the name Anne) is there, standing under an umbrella. Now I just need to use the Dominic System to add the year. I picture former Vice President Al Gore (17 = AG, Al Gore's initials) reclining in a comfy leather chair while getting soaked in the rain (75 = GE, my friend Gerry who used to watch movies in his favourite leather chair, which gives me the prop). I follow the same process for each date and event, posting them at consecutive stages along the route, until finally, in the school hall, I have my friend Julie (July) shaking hands with Olympia Dukakis (OD = 04 for the fourth of the month) on stage at a formal speech ceremony (to denote the declaration of independence). Al Gore (AG = 17) has Gwen Stefani's (76 = GS) feature, which is bleached blond hair, and is standing at the side of the stage.

Reviewing your learning

The "forgetting threshold" (see p.135) – the point at which our spinning memory plates begin to wobble – exists no matter what you're trying to memorize. Whether you're learning information for an exam or to present at an important meeting, knowing when and how to review what you've learned is crucial to ensuring that you minimize any forgetfulness when you're under pressure. The Rule of Five (see pp.76–80) is my favourite method of review, but there are others. Scientists have identified several "effects" of the brain during learning. These can help us to understand why reviewing is so important to effective learning and recall.

The primacy and recency effects

If you try to memorize a list of, say, 20 items without using any strategy, the chances are that the first five to ten items will stick fairly easily. This is known as the primacy effect and it operates because of your patterns of concentration during learning. At the beginning of a list (or any information you're learning), you're more attentive and alert. But then as your brain begins to assimilate that information for storage it's distracted from concentrating on the next wave of information, leading to a sag in learning.

Once you perceive that the information is coming to an end, your concentration levels tend to pick up again, because your brain anticipates the end of the period of concentration, which sort of wakes it up. This is called the recency effect.

The recency effect affects your memory and recall in all sorts of ways. For example, it can significantly influence your memory of things that have happened to you. Imagine that you've had a productive, but unexceptional day at work and are driving through the city to get home. You encounter ten sets of traffic lights. The first seven are green and you go straight through them, but the last three are red and you have to stop. When you get home, your partner asks you how the journey was and what your day was like. Your recent memory is triggered – the journey was slow, because the lights were against you, and generally you've had a bad day. In reality, of course, this is a poor reflection of what actually happened – but it's the idea you have in your head because of your most recent experience.

In a graph that shows attention over the course of time, the primacy and recency effects result in a big sag in concentration in the middle (see graph, p.160), so that recall levels drop to about 25 percent. However, there are various techniques that lecturers or speakers use to ensure that the sag is minimized and that the important information is hammered home. The first is repetition: think of advertising campaigns you hear on the radio or TV – how often do you hear the product name? Usually it's repeated several times, even in a 30-second slot, because your brain absorbs it more willingly if it hears the name more than once.

Another technique often used by speakers or lecturers is to add humour or something off-beat to the talk. An odd shift in pace or content provides a little memory shock, which wakes up your brain cells to keep you alert. The Von Restorff Effect (see pp.65–7) is one such memory shock, and is another great tool to ensure that learning is maximized throughout a speech or lecture.

This is all very well, of course, but it doesn't help if you're learning something from print. In this case, taking regular breaks

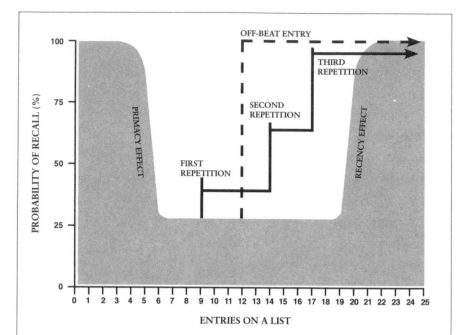

This graph shows what happens to our concentration levels as we're given information. We more easily retain items in a list, for example, at the start of the list (primacy effect) and then at the end of the list (recency effect) than in the middle, where the brain loses focus as it's busy assimilating all that it's already heard. Information (or an entry) that is repeated becomes more memorable with each repetition, and off-beat information "wakes up" the brain (see pp.65–7), making that piece of data stand out, and so more memorable.

is essential. It is much better to divide your time into, say, six 20-minute bursts of study, than to try to focus for a full two hours before taking a break. It stands to reason that short bursts avoid the negative impact of the primacy and recency effects on your ability to retain information (and so recall it).

As a rule of thumb, a 20-minute study period followed by a four- or five-minute break should work well to minimize the influence of primacy and recency. During the mini-rests your memory has a series of reminiscences that consolidate your learning, while you busy yourself with something completely unrelated.

Reviewing the reviews

Whatever you're trying to learn, and for whatever purpose, once you've read the relevant information, distilled it into notes and then memorized it, you need to review it effectively to ensure that it sticks. In 1885, the German psychologist Hermann Ebbinghaus first described the "forgetting curve", which charts the rate at which memory loses data after it has learned something new. The curve reveals that the most rapid memory loss occurs within the first two hours of memorization. In practice, this means that unless you review and refresh your memory regularly during the process of lengthy memorization, you'll have to relearn the information that came first at a later date. As long as you review regularly as you memorize, all the information you learn embeds itself deeply within your memory for better long-term recall.

How to review information effectively

When you read and take notes from a book it's fairly easy to flick back through the pages if you think you might have missed something, but how does this work if you have to review information that you've heard in a meeting or lecture? Perhaps you're attending a training course for your job or are taking exams. Ebbinghaus discovered that if we take notes as we listen, and then review the notes immediately following the event, we can retain 80 percent or more of the information we absorbed. The lecture can be short or long, provided that, after it's finished,

INSIDE MY MIND: WHEN I WAS A STUDENT ...

I remember the run-up to my school exams as weeks of cramming – re-learning information I'd been taught months ago, but had almost entirely forgotten, and trying to memorize other information by rote learning at the last minute. Many of the students I meet these days do exactly the same. I can particularly recall the stress of repeating Spanish words over and over again, in the hope that most would stick long enough to get me through my Spanish oral and vocabulary tests. It's only now (when, obviously, it's too late to make a difference to my grades!) that I realize that revision should be an ongoing process. To excel at what they learn, students need to cast aside the last-minute, damage-limitation exercise and instead go through a process of topping up their learning with patterns of review. That's why I think it's so important to spend time telling you about my review strategies, so that you can apply them to your own learning in your quest for an amazing memory.

the first review of the notes happens straightaway. For optimal recall, he concluded that we should then follow this first review with a second review a day later, a third one a week later, a fourth one a month later, and a fifth, final review three to six months later (if the content was particularly complex). Ebbinghaus called this the "Distributed-Practice Effect" and noted that "with any considerable number of repetitions, a suitable distribution of them over a space of time is decidedly more advantageous than the massing of them at a single time."

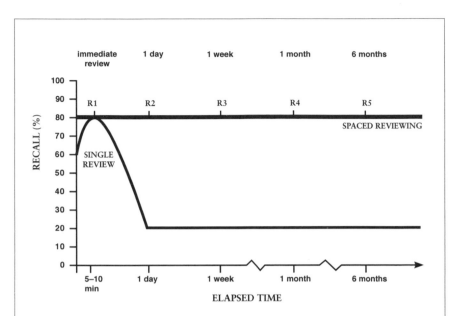

This graph shows what happens when we use a strategy of spaced review, compared with a single review. The latter, performed immediately after learning, shows that recall of the imparted information leaps from 60 to 80 percent. However, if we make no further reviews, within 24 hours recall falls dramatically to only 20 percent, where it stays for the foreseeable future. The information we learned originally would have to be re-learned before we could recall it effectively for, say, an exam. However, if we adopt a spaced review strategy, coming back to the information straightaway, and then a day, a week, a month and six months later, recall can remain at 80 percent, which is what Ebbinghaus called the "Distributed-Practice Effect".

The illustration above shows the Distributed-Practice Effect as a graph. By spacing the reviews of learned information, increasing the intervals of time between each review, recall can remain at levels as high as 80 percent. This means that you don't need to re-learn information when you need to call upon it again, because it's already embedded in your long-term memory.

CHAPTER TWENTY-SEVEN

USING THE TOOLS: EVERYDAY WAYS TO TRAIN YOUR MEMORY

If you want to memorize a deck of cards or learn the Dominic System of a hundred characters and actions, you'll need to designate time to practise. However, once you have the systems in place, everyday situations provide perfect practice sessions for your memory (as well as having practical use). There's no need to delay: begin applying everything you've learned so far to improve both your memory and your efficiency at everyday tasks.

For example, the next time you go shopping, memorize the items in your list rather than writing them down somewhere. The Journey Method is great for this. Choose a journey that you won't confuse with the shopping list – a journey around your home might not work so well, for example, as probably many of the items on the list will be intended for your home, so you may get conflicting images. I think a favourite walk works well, or (for me) a round of golf. Then code the items on the list into the journey. If the first stop is the stile at the entrance to a public footpath, and the first item on your list is a pack of vine tomatoes, perhaps the stile is covered with a vine, dripping with juicy, ripe red fruit. You can smell them as you lean forward to move one of them out of your way to climb over the stile. Perhaps the next stop is a bridge and you need to memorize "avocado" – I would picture the bridge smeared with slippery green avocado flesh, making it hard to walk across. As you do your shopping, all you need to do is mentally walk the journey, recall the images and so bring to mind all the items you need to buy.

Are you a seasoned traveller? I find one of the most infuriating things about arriving at an airport is having to search for a pen to note down where I've parked the car just when I need to be concentrating on where the bus stop is and getting to the terminal in time for my flight. If you use simple mnemonics, you don't need a pen! For example, the last time I flew, I parked in car park C, row 8. In the NATO spelling alphabet, Charlie represents C (Alpha, Bravo, Charlie, Delta, Echo, and so on), so I coded the C using the image of my friend Charlie, and the 8 using number-shapes (a snowman). As I got on the coach, I imagined Charlie building a snowman at the bus stop. The image gave me a little mental shock, because I was off on my hot summer holiday, so the snowman seemed incongruous – even better for memorization.

Once I had checked in, I was told that my flight would be boarding at Gate 34. To memorize this, I created an image of Guy, a friend who used to work in a music shop, running to the gate to catch a plane. This stems from the Dominic System, in which 3 and 4 are represented by the third and fourth letters of the alphabet (C and D). Guy used to sell CDs in a shop and has provided me with a character for that number for many years.

Although these simple scenarios aren't exactly in the same league as memorizing complete decks of cards, when you begin applying the techniques you've learned to everyday tasks, you'll exercise your brain, training it in the art of memory.

Appointments – keeping a mental diary

Another great way to use the techniques you've learned is to keep a mental diary. Most of the time, I have the dates for my work schedule locked in my mind, and I've no need to write them down.

The Dominic System is how I memorize diary dates. Let's say that I receive a booking to give a presentation on the 22nd of the month. Using the Dominic System, the number 22 translates to BB, which for me represents a baby. So, the image of a baby pops into my head as soon as I hear the date. If the appointment is at 11am, I picture the tennis player Andre Agassi (11 = AA) holding the baby. If I already have an appointment that day, I'll already have an image of someone else holding the baby and I'll know straightaway if I'm likely to be overbooking myself.

Remember that coding your numbers into letters is a personal thing. The number 22 gives me baby, but students I've had have used Boris Becker, Bugs Bunny, Bilbo Baggins, Barbara Bush, and a family member or friend with those initials. For the system to work properly, your stepping stones have to be personal to you.

However, this example is all very well if the date is in this month. But what if I have to add the month into the memorization? The months appear to me as the gradient of a hill. January starts low and to my left, and then the gradient starts to climb as it reaches the middle of February and continues to climb through the spring months. It flattens out a little in July for the summer months and then takes a steep incline from September through the months that run up to December. Essentially, I "see" time on the hill – the hill is so well contoured in my mind's eye that I can pinpoint precisely each month. This works for me, but I know from talking to my students and clients that peoples' visual representations of time vary wildly. Some see steps, others a carousel, while still others have no visual representation in their mind at all (in which case seasonal or other triggers or associations, such as Santa Claus for December, might provide a better system: see below).

I "see" the days of the week, too. It's a bit like being on a playground slide. Sunday is where I sit at the top of the slide and I slip down through the weekdays to Friday. Then, Saturday is the ladder I climb to get back to Sunday. Again, my mental picture of the slide is so precise that I can pinpoint every day of the week – for example, I "see" Wednesday half way down. But, this is entirely personal and, like the months, it may or may not help you – you need to search your own mind for a representation that triggers each day. It may be a slide, or a hill, or a roundabout. If my visual systems don't work for you at all, try the following.

• Word–sound associations

Let's say you're invited to a birthday party on Wednesday March 28. Using the Dominic System, I convert 28 to BH. You might picture the legendary singer Buddy Holly **march**ing (March) **forward** into the party with guitar in hand and singing one of his popular songs. I get Wednesday from "forward", because Wednesday is the fourth day of the week.

• Picture-key associations

Coding the months into picture keys is also effective. To remind you that your daughter is appearing in the school Nativity on December 21 you might imagine the actor Ben Affleck (21 = BA) turning up at school dressed as Santa Claus. In this case, it's not the slope of a hill that gives December, but the picture key of Santa. If you need to memorize that the date is a Thursday, you could add an image of Santa being struck by lightning (my image for Thursday is the Norse god of thunder and lightning, Thor, from whom the day gets its name).

Incidentally, to memorize the start time, I use the 24-hour clock combined with the Dominic System. So, if the play starts at 3.30pm, I convert this to 1530, which I break up into pairs according to the Dominic System: AE (=15) + CO (=30). I use a complex image to put Albert Einstein hosting a chat show (my action for Conan O'Brien) on the stage of my daughter's school.

Here's a complete list of my picture-key associations for the months of the year and the days of the week.

MONTHS

January	Jan, Jenny
February	Fab Four (the Beatles)
March	Marching soldiers
April	Rain, Umbrella (April showers)
May	Maypole
June	June, or sand dune
July	Julie Walters (actress)
August	Lion (from the star sign Leo)

September	Leaves falling (fall season)
October	Octopus
November	Novice priest, a book (novel)
December	Santa Claus, Declan Donnelly (UK TV presenter)

DAYS

Sunday	Sun, Sunday newspapers
Monday	Money
Tuesday	Twins ("twos")
Wednesday	Bride (at a wedding)
Thursday	Thunder, Thor
Friday	Fried egg
Saturday	Saturn's rings

Now that you have the tools for memorizing your appointments, try the exercise on the following page.

Keeping up with conversation

Although I was told I had dyslexia as a child, I believe a more accurate diagnosis of my condition would have been Attention Deficit Disorder. I couldn't keep my attention on anything I was taught – I used to watch my teachers' lips move, and I knew they were speaking, but my mind was far away in an imaginary world that took me anywhere but the classroom. You might not have been like that at school, but I suspect there are very few people in the world who could say that they have never tuned out during a meeting, a lecture or even perhaps a particularly boring play, show or concert.

EXERCISE 14: Keeping a Mental Diary

Use your imagination to memorize the following. At first, try your memory skills on just the dates and events. Test yourself by trying to recall each event when you can see only the dates column. When you feel confident, try the exercise again, adding in the day and time, too. Once you've finished memorizing, cover everything but the dates and test your recall of the events, days and times. Score one point for each correct event, day and time (maximum three points per date). A score of 7–10 is good; 11–15 is excellent. (I've left the events out of chronological order, as appointments rarely come up in a timeline.)

DATE	EVENT	DAY	TIME
October 16	Dalí exhibition	Wednesday	7pm
May 31	Bank manager	Friday	3pm
August 8	Theatre	Saturday	7.30pm
April 22	Dentist	Wednesday	4.15pm
March 13	Optician	Monday	9.20am

As an extra test, cover the page and answer these questions:

- Who are you booked to see on May 31 and at what time?
- What are the date, day and time of your visit to the Dalí exhibition?
- What is happening on August 8?
- What are the date, day and time of your dental appointment?
- What are the date, day and time of your eye test?

I'm slightly embarrassed to say that my inability to concentrate extended to conversations with my friends and family, too. For years, until I was well into teenager-hood, I was described as "Dreamy old Dom". It's hard to explain, but it didn't feel voluntary. I wasn't conscious that I was becoming absent from a conversation – it just happened. Even if I tried to stay in tune, my mind would wander. Keeping track of a conversation is a wonderful skill to have, no matter what you do (for example, politicians and lawyers need it to be good at their jobs; the rest of us should behave like this for simple good manners!). And it's also a great way to practise your memory skills in everyday life.

Years of scientific study have shown that, compared with the brains of non-ADD sufferers, people with Attention Defiicit Disorder have decreased electrical activity in the prefrontal lobe of the brain and slow cortical blood flow. It's believed that these are the reasons that ADD sufferers find it so hard to concentrate.

Today, doctors prescribe stimulant medication to try to control the condition in children. The aim is to speed up the brain's activity just enough to promote attention and concentration, but not so much as to provoke any erratic behaviour.

The medication isn't a cure, but it does seem to alleviate the symptoms of ADD. However, the drugs weren't around in my day, and I believe I've overcome my condition purely as a result of training my memory. These days I'm able to listen to and retain the content of a conversation or meeting, no matter how dreary it may be. There are times when I do zone out – as do we all – but the difference is that I have a choice in the matter. In other words, I zone out because I want to, not because I can't stop it happening.

There are two things going on here. First, I believe that training my memory has increased my powers of concentration. But also, I'm able to use my memory skills specifically to stay tuned in to the details of the information I'm being given. But how?

As you're listening to someone speak, try to encapsulate segments of the conversation and convert them into key images. Then, anchor the images in your mind in the correct order – for a short conversation the number–shape system works best, I think (as we'll see in a moment), although you may prefer to use a journey (I use journeys for meetings or longer conversations). If the conversation has numbers in it, or facts and figures, you can use any of the mnemonic systems in this book – including the Dominic System – to work the information into the memorization.

The number–shape system may be used as follows. Let's say my PA calls me about a meeting I'm to have with a client. To memorize the information she gives me without need of pen or paper, I mentally number each detail. Each number becomes a number–shape that gives me the position of the detail and something that can interact with the association for the detail itself. Essentially, I use the number–shapes as hooks on which to hang the information in the correct order. Here's an example:

"Hi Dominic, I've just got confirmation of the hotel you're staying at tonight. It's the Victoria Hotel in Bury Street."

1   I picture Queen Victoria holding a candle standing by an open grave. My number–shape for 1 is a candle and the open grave obviously helps me to remember the name of the street.

"When you get there, ask at reception for your client, Mr Taylor. He is taking you to lunch where you can discuss the contract."

2   I imagine a swan (number–shape for 2) with a tape measure around its neck. I always associate the name Taylor with a tape measure (such as a tailor would use).

"Just for your information, Mr Taylor is a keen clay pigeon shooter and his favourite restaurant is the Coconut Grove and that's where he's taking you."

3   My image is of my client in handcuffs (my number–shape for 3) as I imagine myself shooting coconuts from the sky.

"As soon as you have agreed a price with Mr Taylor, I'd like you to send me a text message to the number 3512."

4   I picture myself in a boat (number–shape for 4), with Clint Eastwood (35 = CE), wielding a sword. Clint is using the action of Antonio Banderas (12 = AB), star of the film *The Mask of Zorro*.

I'm able to construct these images in my mind instantaneously – but that comes only with practice. Have a go at memorizing the key points of the next conversation you have. As you do so, not only will you be making sure that you can impress the person who was talking to you by recalling everything they've said: you'll also be getting in some valuable memory practice.

CHAPTER TWENTY-EIGHT

USING THE TOOLS: JUST FOR FUN

We've talked about the serious side of training your memory – the boost to your confidence and self-esteem, the improvements to your creativity, and so on, and we've also talked about how you can apply the techniques to make your everyday life easier. However, having an amazing memory is also a lot of fun. Party tricks for your friends are not only a great way to show off your memory power, but also a perfect opportunity to practise. I often go to functions or parties at which I know I'm going to be asked to perform some feat of memory to wow the guests – here are some of my favourite memory tricks, just for fun.

Pick a card ... any card

The obvious trick for me to begin with at any party is a card trick. You have to have memorized a deck of cards using the Journey Method before you arrive and you have to resist the urge to ask someone to shuffle (have some quips up your sleeve to bat away any hecklers who want to take the cards from you to mix them up). Take the deck from your pocket and fan it out face down. Ask someone to take a random card from the fanned deck. As they remove the card, take a peek at the card on top of the one they removed. Let's say, you peek at the Queen of Clubs. Scan your pre-loaded journey to find your character for the Queen of Clubs, then walk one stage further on to find the card that's been removed from the deck. Announce your answer.

If you get good at this, you can try a variation. Allow someone to cut the deck (cut, but not shuffle!). As long as you take a peek at the new card at the bottom of the deck, you can amaze your audience by telling them that you know what the new top card is – declare it, and let someone else turn it over to gasps of admiration. In theory you can go on reciting card after card, in order, all the way through the deck from this point. All you have to do is start your journey from the position of the new top card, rather than from the original first card in the deck. (If you want to be really convincing, at the start of the trick ask people to keep cutting the deck – as long as you keep track of the bottom card and don't change the sequence of the cards within each cut, you'll still be able to recite the cards in order.)

One other card trick is to identify a missing card from the deck. You memorize your deck, as previously, before the party, then with your back turned you ask someone to remove one card from the deck, without disturbing the other cards. They put the card in their pocket, out of your sight. Turn around and ask the person to turn over each card in the deck slowly, one on top of the other, in front of you. In your mind, as the other person deals the cards, you mentally walk through your journey – when you hit the missing card, you'll know because you'll be expecting it to appear on the next stage of your journey, but in fact the dealt cards will skip a stage. Don't reveal your answer until all the cards have been dealt, to prolong the suspense!

Literary genius

People have come to expect me to memorize a deck of cards, or names and faces, but one of my favourite party tricks is a little more unusual. If you want to really baffle your audience, memorize the contents of a book – or at least appear to.

First, I ask my host to give me a book of around 100 pages in length. I take the book, turn over the pages one by one, and after five or six minutes I hand the book back to a guest for safe keeping. I claim that I have read through the entire book and have committed its contents to memory. I ask the guest to come back to me in an hour or so with the book in hand along with anyone who wants to see my memory in action. Later on, I ask the guest to read me the first few lines from a randomly chosen page in the book. The lines are read to me and then I tell the eager guests what page that text falls on.

How is it done? Well, as I turn over the pages when I'm given the book, I memorize a single word on the first line of each page, beginning at page one. I scan the top line on every page to spot a word that I think will easily form a strong, individual image. Using the Journey Method (I need a journey or journeys with as many stages as there are pages in the book), I anchor the images, in order, to the stages along my route. In order for the trick to work, page one of the book has to correspond to stage one on the journey, page two to stage two, and so on, so that I can use the numerical position of the image to give me the page number.

During the time the book is with the guest for safe-keeping, I make a quick review of the key words and their corresponding key images, so that I'm confident that I can perform the trick.

Of course, to perform the trick well, you need to know your journeys backwards and forwards and the numerical position of key stages in relation to the other stages of the journey. If you use two 50-stage journeys back to back, to give you the 100 stages, you need to be practised at translating the second set of 50 stages into the higher page numbers.

You don't need to know the exact numerical position of every stage, though, as long as you have key markers. For example, along the route I generally use for this trick, I know instantly what the 1st, 5th, 11th, 13th, 15th, 21st and 26th stages are. One, 5 and 15 seem logical markers to have, then 11 stands out to me because the two 1s looks like railings, while 13 is "unlucky" and 21 is the "key to the door", so these stick in my mind, too. Finally, 26 represents the half-way point in a card deck. From these markers I can walk forwards or backwards to the page number I need.

For example, let's say that I've used my preferred book journey, which travels around a village I lived in as a child. It starts from our old house, crosses heathland to a village inn, then leads to a cricket pitch and ends up inside a village hall. There are 100 stages in all. If someone reads the first line of a page at random and I register the word "violin", the image of the violin immediately pops up in my head at the relevant stage – let's say it's propped up against the oak tree that's my stage shortly before I get to the cricket pitch. I know that the pitch is stage 21 on my journey, and that the tree is two stages before that. If I take two steps back from the cricket pitch, I'm at stage 19. So, the word violin appears on page 19. I've worked back two stops from the closest marker, rather than walking forwards through the 19 stages from the beginning of the journey. Voilà! The quicker you can become at coming up with the answer, the more impressive the trick.

Once you get really adept at this, you can post two images at each stage of the journey, so that you can memorize bigger books. However, always make sure that each pair of images interact in the right order. So, if the key words from consecutive pages are "soup" and "frog", I imagine soup being poured over the frog; but if the order were "frog" then "soup", I imagine the frog jumping into the soup. The first word from the pair of pages is always the subject and the second is always the object of the image I place along the route. Although this sounds complicated, it didn't take me long to master – I just had to make sure I'd organized my routes well and had had a bit of practice at the maths involved with placing two images (two pages) at each stage of the journey.

It's also possible (and perhaps more impressive) to reverse the trick so that I give a summary of what's on the page if someone gives me the page number. It takes a little more time, because I need to read more of the text on each page to get a sense of the story. Once I have my overview for the page, I code that into a general scene to place along the journey. When someone gives me the page number, I can give a summary of that page's content.

It takes some practice to become really slick at this, but I promise you it's worth it for the impact on your delighted audience. Start with just 30 pages or so of a book at first and work up to a whole novel as you gain in confidence and skill.

CHAPTER TWENTY-NINE

AGE EQUALS EXPERIENCE, NOT FORGETFULNESS!

I was 34 years old when I entered the first World Memory Championships, back in 1991. I believe that my memory is in a much better state than it was 20 years ago. I am now in my 54th year, and while many of my peers are complaining that their memory is starting to deteriorate, I certainly can't say the same. I believe that my constant work with memory techniques – whether I'm teaching, coaching, performing or competing – has kept my powers of recall and concentration in fantastic shape. In fact, I would even go so far as to say that my memory is still improving.

So, if you're wondering whether or not it's true that, as we age, our cognitive abilities start to decline, it will be quite clear to you that as far as I'm concerned this is nonsense. In my opinion a fading memory has to do with lack of motivation (perhaps boredom with life, or feeling depressed), anxiety, and general poor health – but it's not to do with the actual hardware of your brain.

Since 1986 the epidemiologist David Snowden has been tracking the lives of 678 elderly nuns in Minnesota to try to measure the effects of ageing on mental fitness. The volunteers are aged between 75 and 104, and because they all share the same living conditions, they make an ideal study group.

Perhaps unsurprisingly, Snowden found that a healthy diet was directly linked to healthy ageing and longevity. In addition, the nuns with a positive attitude to life had a decreased risk of age-related mental difficulties. However, his most striking discovery was that there's a correlation between an enquiring mind and reduced incidence of Alzheimer's. In particular, nuns who were able, from an early age, to read and write, and who expressed themselves well both orally and in writing, lived longer and were less prone to dementia. Regular mental and physical exercise also played a significant part, as did a keenness to read and be involved in the community.

As with all the other parts of your body, to be healthy your brain needs you to follow the general principles of a good, healthy lifestyle. Physical exercise, good nutrition, intellectual stimulation, and making time for relaxation, all play their part in ensuring that you stay mentally pin-sharp.

Your brain needs ... oxygen

Your brain can't operate without oxygen, and this means that your circulation has to be in prime condition. Exercise is by far the best method to boost your circulation and get the brain fully oxygen-fed. Countless studies provide evidence to show that exercise improves brain function, but I also know from personal experience that if I feel physically fit when I enter the World Memory Championships, I can enjoy much deeper levels of concentration and I have far more energy to keep me going through the (now) three days of gruelling mental challenges. The techniques in this book, if put into practice, can significantly increase the efficiency of your memory. However, if you combine your mental training with physical exercise, too, you'll ramp up the speed with which your memory functions. If you like, the memory techniques are the software for your brain, but the hardware, your body, needs to be in good shape so that the software can work properly.

Exercise in my life doesn't mean pumping iron – that's not for me. I might walk miles every week on the golf course and I take my dog for daily walks, but when I'm training for a memory competition, I run. In the short term, running regulates my breathing to ensure that my brain and muscles get ample oxygen, and also releases feel-good hormones (endorphins), which help to keep me relaxed (see below) and positive. Some studies show that, in the long term, forms of aerobic exercise – including running – that leave you slightly breathless can help to nourish your brain cells. Furthermore, a study on mice, conducted at the University of Cambridge in 2010, concluded that running may encourage new brain cells to form, increasing the size of your brain, specifically in the region of the hippocampus – the part associated with memory and learning (see p.64).

When I'm training for a memory competition, I have a light, energy-packed breakfast (such as a small bowl of porridge) and then I run for about 30 minutes, three or four times a week. I always time my runs to get a measure of my fitness – the faster I can do the distance, the fitter I know I'm getting. (See pages 188–9 for a full example of my training diary.)

Dr Gunther Karsten, the German Memory Champion and a winner of the World Memory Championships, takes physical training enormously seriously as part of his brain-training regime. In his words, "70 percent of my preparation is memory training, the other 30 percent of my time I designate to working out my body." This master memorizer cycles, plays tennis and soccer, performs sits-ups and chin-ups, lifts weights, and does track running to keep his body *and* his brain in shape.

You don't have to do quite that much, of course, but to keep your memory in top condition it's a good idea to find a form of exercise that suits you and make it a regular part of your routine. In general, 20 to 30 minutes of exercise that increases your heart rate enough to leave you slightly breathless, two or three times a week, is a good place to start – if you can do more, the whole of you will benefit, including your amazing brain.

Your brain needs ... calm

Think about how your head feels when you're stressed. If you're like me, you have a sense of almost madness, of so much going on that you can't think clearly. Now imagine feeling like that and then going into a memory competition. This can't be allowed to happen! There's ample scientific explanation for the effects of stress on brain function (and specifically memory). Stress hormones, particularly cortisol (also known as hydrocortisone), inhibit the growth of new brain cells. The hippocampal region of your brain – the part related to memory – is one of the few brain regions that can grow new cells, so stress has a direct effect on your ability to memorize and recall.

There are several ways I reduce the effects of stress on my body. The first, and for me the most important, is regular exercise (see above). Physical activity reduces the production of stress hormones and also releases powerful mood-enhancing endorphins, which provide a feel-good factor that keeps my head clear and my confidence at top levels. I've learned throughout my life that a little bit of confidence can go a long way on the path toward success – and often, with such high-class competition at memory championships these days, the difference between first prize and runner-up can come down purely to how confident you're feeling on the day. Although the logic is somewhat circular, I also use the Journey Method to help me relax. Any activity that fully engages your brain and encourages it to tune out of the constant, nagging internal babble that so often is the cause of stress is a great way to bring on a state of calm. For me, a few rounds of memorizing cards using the Journey Method does just that.

Finally, one of my favourite ways to relax is through music – I play the piano and have a mini-recording studio at home, where I write and record my own tunes.

Your brain needs ... good food

The food you eat supplies your brain with essential nutrients to keep your neurons firing so that they can communicate efficiently with one another. The key brain nutrients are omega-3 and omega-6 fatty acids (so-called essential fats, which can't be derived from any source other than food), as well as B-vitamins, choline and vitamin C, the three of which together help the body to produce the neurotransmitter acetylcholine. Studies show that the body's production line of acetylcholine is often damaged in patients with Alzheimer's Disease, which suggests that this chemical compound has a strong link with the efficiency of your memory.

Eggs, poultry, avocados, flaxseed and pumpkin seeds are among the best sources of omega-6 fats, while oily fish, such as salmon, tuna and mackerel, and most nut oils, provide good amounts of omega-3. I try to eat oily fish two or three times a week (often with salad for lunch), and I snack on nuts and seeds, rather than chocolate or crisps, both of which are high in saturated fat – an unhealthy form of fat, believed to hamper motivation and lower intelligence. Oily fish and eggs are also good sources of choline. Other good sources include cauliflower, almonds and soya.

The B-vitamins (particularly B1, B5 and B12) appear to improve overall brain function, including memory. Lack of B-vitamins can also lead to low mood, anxiety and depression. A diet that is rich in a wide range of fruits and vegetables should give good levels of all the B-vitamins you need, as will tuna, turkey, Brazil nuts, and pulses, such as chickpeas. However, you could also take a B-complex supplement, as I do, to top up. Buy the best brand you can afford and follow the manufacturer's instructions on dosage.

Fruits and vegetables play another important role in a healthy diet. When the body metabolizes food to provide energy, the food undergoes oxidation, which produces free radicals, by-products that break down the body's cells causing ageing and some serious diseases (such as cancer), and destroying brain cells. However, help is at hand: free radicals are neutralized by foods rich in antioxidants, in particular the vitamins A, C and E (I think of the ACE of Hearts to help me remember), and the minerals zinc

INSIDE MY MIND: HERBS FOR NEURONS

I'm a huge fan of Ginkgo biloba, *a herbal extract that research shows can improve circulation to the brain. Ginkgo is a vasodilator – it dilates the blood vessels to allow blood to flow more freely through your body's circulatory system and inhibits chemicals that thicken the blood, again improving blood flow. If the flow of blood to the brain is improved, more oxygen and essential nutrients are transported there, so the brain is nourished more effectively. Ginkgo is also a powerful antioxidant, helping to deactivate the free radicals that can destroy the body's cells and contribute to ageing. I prefer to take the herb in capsule form, but it's available as tablets, too. I buy the best-quality extract I can lay my hands on – as with most things in life, you get what you pay for.*

and selenium. Blackberries, blueberries, broccoli, plums, prunes, raisins, raspberries, spinach and strawberries are all good sources of antioxidants – and some of my favourites!

Your brain needs ... moderation

No one likes a killjoy, but I believe that to keep your brain working at its best requires moderation. Alcohol, for example, is an arch enemy of your brain power. Regularly drinking to excess inhibits the functioning of your hippocampus, which means that your memory suffers as a direct consequence of the alcohol you consume. When I'm not training for a memory championship, I enjoy the odd glass or two of Sauvignon Blanc; but during training

186 YOU CAN HAVE AN AMAZING MEMORY

– that is, for at least two months before a competition – I abstain entirely from alcohol.

Your brain needs ... things to do

Young or old, your brain needs stimulation if it's to function at its best. This is as true for children as it is for the rest of us in our 20s, 30s, 40s and beyond. My parents always gave me toys that nurtured my innate spirit of enquiry and discovery. They were careful to provide me with activities to expand, rather than merely entertain, my mind. Meccano®, LEGO®, puzzles, colouring pens, plasticine, a chemistry set, and (perhaps unsurprisingly) a deck of cards allowed for endless hours of stimulating play.

I remember, when I was aged about six years old, asking my mother if she would buy me a shiny, colourful, wind-up toy that I had spotted in a store window. She didn't buy it for me – but she was careful to explain why. She told me that the toy wound up, ran its course and then stopped – and that's all it did. She reasoned that I'd be bored with it after a few goes. She was right, and I knew it. I was much better off with toys that held my attention because they required some real input from my brain.

In adulthood, I have my wonderful job – the game of memory – to keep my brain in tone. Best of all, I shall continue to strive for the level of excellence that keeps me ahead of my competitors, which means that memory techniques and all the exercises I do to keep my mind agile never stop, unlike that wind-up toy.

Although there are dozens of brain-training games on the market, studies reveal no hard evidence that the improvements to your learning capacity using a console is transferable to everyday life (that is, consoles appear to improve only your ability to play the games). There's really only one tool you need to give your brain a thorough workout, and that's a deck of cards. If you want to exercise your brain fully, use my techniques to learn to memorize a deck of cards – and then keep practising. Every time you have another go, you'll strengthen the neural pathways to improve the functioning of your whole brain, not just your memory.

If I feel a bit sluggish, or as though my mind is a bit foggy, I take a deck, memorize it and note my time for both memorizing and recall. I then have a firm indication of whether the motor in my head is firing on all cylinders. If it's not – if recall is a bit slow or if I make mistakes – I get myself back into training (see pp.188–9) to make sure that I don't let my mental acuity slip too far.

Your brain needs ... a good night's sleep

Sleep is essential for the proper functioning of your memory. An article published in *Nature* magazine in 2010 concluded that during sleep your brain consolidates its learning from the day before. Another study, conducted at the University of Chicago, has indicated that during sleep the brain establishes and reinforces neural pathways to link memories and learning together. The research seems to show that sleep enables the brain to catch thoughts, memories and other elements of learning that may have seemed lost during the day. In practice, it's that feeling of something coming to you during the night – you know, the thing you had struggled to remember during the day. Your brain, in its most relaxed state, allows those pathways to open and memories that you thought were lost, to surface.

INSIDE MY MIND: A WEEK IN MY LIFE

As I said at the beginning of this chapter, I believe that my memory today is as good as, if not better than, it's ever been, because I exercise my brain every day. Not only that, I look after my physical health, too. The following is a summary of a typical week of memory training for me.

SUNDAY
Morning: EEG testing (see p.114) to measure my brainwave frequencies and the balance between the two hemispheres. Run 3.2km (2 miles). Afternoon: Two five-minute memorizations of 400 numbers.

MONDAY
Morning: 20-minute session on the AVS machine (see pp.119–20) to balance the electrical activity in my brain. Follow-up EEG testing. Afternoon: Timed memorization of ten separate, shuffled decks of cards.

TUESDAY
Morning: Run 3.2km (2 miles). Afternoon: Memorize as many random words as possible in 15 minutes.

WEDNESDAY
Morning: Round of golf. One hour memorizing numbers – aiming for around 2,400 digits in 60 minutes. Afternoon: Visit a public gardens or go for an interesting walk to look

for potential new journeys. I use a video camera to film possible routes, which enables me to review the journey at a later date if need be.

THURSDAY

Morning: Run 3.2km (2 miles).
Afternoon: Names and faces practice, using the Internet or faces I find in magazines and newspapers.

FRIDAY

Morning: 30-minutes' practice of binary numbers, as well as speed memorization of ten decks of cards.
Afternoon: Training review – I check back over my times for the week to ensure I'm making progress as the training intensifies.

SATURDAY

Morning: Run 3.2km (2 miles).
Afternoon: 15 minutes' memorization of abstract images and five minutes of fictional dates and events.

As well as the specific memory training, every morning I have a bowl of cereal (such as muesli) or porridge for breakfast. My lunches and suppers tend to be light and healthy – grilled fish or poultry with vegetables or salad and some fruit. I try to steer clear of saturated fats, such as crisps and cakes, as much as I can, but I do treat myself to a curry once a week. And, of course, I limit my alcohol or avoid it altogether.

CHAPTER THIRTY

I'VE DONE ALL THAT, NOW WHAT CAN I EXPECT?

All the techniques I've taught you and the practice sessions I've suggested can, used regularly and with some degree of dedication, give you a perfect memory. However, memory training also offers so much more. I discovered this as a by-product of trying to push my memory to its limits. Although it's been incredible to have become a multiple World Memory Champion, it's really only because of the "add-ons" that I believe memory training has changed my life. Here are some of the amazing things that I believe can happen to you as a result of having an amazing memory.

Improved fluid intelligence

In the 20th century, British-born psychologist Raymond Cattell identified that human intelligence can be divided broadly into two categories: crystallized and fluid. Crystallized intelligence comes from information that you've set about learning – knowledge that you've deliberately intended to acquire. Fluid intelligence, on the other hand, is more intangible. It's the intelligence that derives from intuition, reasoning and logic. The more honed your fluid intelligence, the more able you are to reason quickly, think abstractly and solve problems in creative, imaginative ways, without necessarily using acquired knowledge.

A good way to think of the difference between the two is to imagine what happens when a child learns something new. If a child learns to count to ten in French, say, that provides a new piece of crystallized intelligence. Despite that new piece of learning, the child's fluid intelligence, which is innate and distinct from learning, remains unchanged.

Studies show that we use our fluid intelligence in a wide variety of cognitive tasks and that it's critical to our success at work and in education, especially when the task in hand involves the need to solve complex problems. It is usually measured by tracking performance in psychometric testing – recognizing sequences in patterns and so on. Although we can become accustomed to these sorts of test by doing them often, practising doesn't actually have very much influence over improving fluid intelligence at all. And that's why memory training with regard to improving fluid intelligence is so special.

Training your short-term (working) memory and accessing your fluid intelligence uses some of the same areas of the brain, so memory training can have a big impact on fluid intelligence. The more you train, the greater the gains in your ability to apply logic and reasoning and the more acute your intuition.

This is especially good news if you're worried about the common belief that your working memory declines with age (although I hope I've allayed your fears already). If you train your memory regularly, evidence suggests that your fluid intelligence will stay young, despite the passing years.

Greater powers of concentration

One of the most difficult disciplines for me at the World Memory Championships is trying to memorize a 100-digit number spoken at the rate of one digit per second. The adjudicator reads each digit only once, so if a competitor becomes distracted and loses concentration, even for a second, the round is lost. I've already mentioned that the Dominic who went to school was pretty hopeless at concentrating for anything more than a few minutes at a time. Training my memory, especially for events such as the Spoken Number round at the Championships, has provided me with the necessary levels of mental discipline to concentrate for hours at a time.

The skill has been transferable, too – now I'm more than able to concentrate on a lecture, or on something someone is telling me, even over a prolonged period. I can switch my concentration off, if I want to – and then I can turn it back on at will. I believe that memory training in even small ways – such as memorizing a shopping list or where you parked the car – makes you more attentive. It switches on the light, if you like.

If, like me, you've suffered from ADD or other attention problems, I'm certain that my memory techniques will help you learn to enter the "zone" or "flow" and activate your concentration (and deactivate it at will, if you like). If you've always been able to concentrate well, the techniques can only improve and hone your natural abilities.

Gaining a skill for life

I'm happy to say that all the work you've done throughout this book will stay with you for ever. Once you've trained your memory so that you can achieve feats of memorization, you've reached such a level of attainment that you'll never lose the skill.

Of course, you'll need to practise to get the pathways firmly established – no one became an expert in anything from simply reading a book and then putting it down and forgetting about everything it said. If you want to be a champion at anything, you have to be hungry for it, persistent in your efforts to attain it, and prepared to put in the hours of training.

However, as I've already said, the great thing about memory training is that you can find everyday situations to give yourself a daily mental workout (see pp.164–73). Of course, rather like riding a bicycle, if you don't practise for a while, you might wobble a bit the next time you try it – but the basic skills will always be with you.

When I haven't competed in memory sports for a few years, I've noticed that the speed at which I can memorize information slows down a bit. But I'm still able to perform feats of memory with relative ease. With a little bit of training, returning to – and winning – competitive memory sports is always within my grasp.

So, if you haven't managed to practise for a while, don't imagine that the pathways you've laid down so far will become overgrown. All the work you've done is still with you. I encourage you to add to it as often as you can, safe in the knowledge that each time you achieve a new feat of memorization, you will have built on the skill you're acquiring for life.

CHAPTER THIRTY-ONE

LOOK AT WHAT YOU CAN DO NOW!

So, I've given you the methods and you've put them into practice by memorizing shopping lists, to-do lists, your work diary, PINs and all the other things that you can use your memory for in your everyday life. With all those memory workouts going on, you've been giving your brain lots of essential exercise to take it to its peak performance.

Now it's time to measure your progress with some further memory tests (see pp.196–201). The first two tests are similar to those at the beginning of the book, when you took your first baseline measurements. The purpose of these is to give you an idea of how much you've improved since those first scores, before you had the benefit of my techniques to work with.

To offer you some encouragement, and some belief in what you've learned already, I can tell you that once I've taught students (who range in age from ten to 17 years old) the Link Method, I see an immediate increase in their scores for word memorization. Once they've learned number–shapes, I see a small improvement in number memorization. But once I've explained the Dominic System and how to use it with the Journey Method, students make a huge leap, becoming able to memorize 80 or more numbers in about 15 minutes. Surprisingly, many of them start to achieve these scores after just a couple of weeks of training.

Remember, these tests are merely indicators for how well you're applying the methods you've learned. I'm not aiming to teach you to memorize long lists of numbers or words, but to hand over methods for developing a powerful memory that you can apply in practical ways in all walks of your life. My students tell me that that's exactly what *they* do – and they assure me that it works.

I hope that if you've followed the systems and become confident with each method before moving on to the next, you'll see massive improvement in your scores – just like my students. This being the case, I also wanted to give you the opportunity to try some exercises that should really stretch you. So, after the measurement tests, I've given you three more exercises that are very similar to the heats in the World Memory Championships. Don't be disheartened if you find these exercises tricky – they're intended to be! My guess, though, is that with a little bit of practice, you'll be amazed at how well you can do.

EXERCISE 15: Redrawing the Baseline

TEST 1: Three-minute words

Using the strategy that works best for you, memorize this list of 30 words in sequence (reading down the columns from left to right). As you did at the start of the book, set a timer so that you don't have to clock-watch. You have 3 minutes for the memorization and as long as you need for the recall. Write the words as you recall them on a sheet of paper, then look back at the list to see how well you did. Score one point for each word in the correct order. Deduct a mark for words that are in the wrong order. Two words round the wrong way, counts as two positional errors, so deduct two marks, but then resume point-scoring from the next correct word. If you managed to memorize only, say, 15 items in the time, your maximum score is 15 (that is, don't deduct points for words not memorized).

BISCUIT	SKULL	DIARY
TREASURE	WHEELCHAIR	BEARD
ICER	LADDER	TEACHER
HOUND	DRESS	ANCHOR
FLUTE	FLOWERS	WISHBONE
NICKEL	BABY	FILE
SANDWICH	LAWNMOWER	WHIP
TEASPOON	TARGET	CARTOON
ATLAS	IGLOO	BLOOD
SKI	ONION	MOTH

How did you do? Any score above 15 is great – and if you scored in the 20s, you should be really proud of what you've achieved. If you scored fewer than 15 – don't despair. Your associations aren't strong enough yet, and you just need to keep practising so that you make strong links that resonate deeply in your mind. Find ways to practise your memory techniques in your everyday life (see pp.164–73).

TEST 2: Three-minute numbers

Again, using any method you like, memorize the following 30 numbers, reading left to right, in 3 minutes. Score a point for a correct number in the correct position, and deduct a point for misplacing a number (again, two numbers round the wrong way counts as two positional errors, so you would deduct two points, and so on).

4	2	1	6	6	3	0	0	7	1
9	5	8	0	4	5	5	9	2	7
3	8	1	1	2	9	3	4	5	7

How does your score compare with your first attempt at number memorization at the beginning of the book? If you scored 15 or above this time round, you've clearly got the hang of how to turn lists of numbers into items that are more memorable. Keep going until you get all the numbers right. Again, if you didn't score as well as you'd hoped – persevere. Perfection will come with practice.

Advanced Memory Tests

TEST 1: Five-minute words

You have 5 minutes to memorize as many words, in order (reading down the columns), as possible, and as long as you need for recall. Score one point for each word recalled in the right position. Deduct ten points for

ZIP	BILL	CROW
INDUSTRY	ZINC	GLADIATOR
LATCH	AGRICULTURIST	AVENDER
BAR	CAMEL	MANOR
EXTINGUISHER	YEAST	PLINTH
COMET	STORK	AUTUMN
PETAL	COT	FALCON
DEGREE	FUNGUS	INTERNET
CART	APPLE	DOCTOR
HULL	COMIC	UMBRELLA
WASP	BANK	IMPORT
EXHIBIT	AEROSOL	ROULETTE
SPANIEL	ABBEY	TARPAULIN
TOY	EQUATOR	DIGIT
SPROUT	GUTTER	GEOLOGIST
PERSON	DOT	RAPIER
LOLLIPOP	TINSEL	GASTRONOMY
ASP	SILHOUETTE	HOIST
ARROW	NICHE	TEMPLE
MAJOR	MANDARIN	WOODPECKER

one error in a column; lose the whole column for two or more errors. A score of 20 is good; 30 or more is excellent. The best score for this test at the UK Open Championships stands at 70 points.

REMEDY	SOAP
ACCORDION	LASER
ROCK	GEYSER
BEAST	URN
FACT	OPAL
HARPOON	RHUBARB
INFLATE	PARROT
DACHSHUND	SUBMARINE
HORNET	TEETH
IMP	APOSTROPHE
POLL	AQUEDUCT
DIRT	PROSECUTE
DIAL	INTERLUDE
BEAVER	GERBIL
HANDKERCHIEF	COLANDER
INCA	SEWER
EXAMPLE	BULLDOG
ADDER	GARGOYLE
WEASEL	COMPASS
IGUANA	ILLUSION

Advanced Memory Tests (continued)

TEST 2: Five-minute speed numbers

You have 5 minutes to memorize as many numbers as possible, in order, row by row. Score one point for each correct number in the correct position. For one mistake in a row, deduct 20 digits; for two or more mistakes in a row, deduct the whole row. The maximum score is 440. A score of 20–30 is good; a score of 31–40 is excellent; more than 40 makes you a potential champion. The World Record stands at 405.

```
3 4 8 3 1 1 3 9 5 8 5 7 6 7 8 5 2 7 7 3 1 5 1 6 6 4 7 2 8 0 3 5 0 6 1 9 3 5 9 7
8 5 6 8 4 6 0 5 3 5 6 1 2 3 1 8 2 8 5 8 8 5 6 5 0 4 4 3 5 7 4 9 3 0 1 6 0 3 9 7
0 2 0 1 2 9 9 6 8 4 4 9 4 0 5 0 2 9 7 1 3 7 4 9 5 3 8 2 6 3 4 2 3 9 9 2 5 0 3 1
0 2 2 2 9 9 8 5 1 1 3 8 4 2 5 4 4 6 2 0 5 4 7 2 9 4 0 6 9 4 0 4 1 9 7 4 6 6 1 0
9 1 2 9 7 3 7 5 0 4 1 9 1 3 9 6 9 7 8 7 3 0 5 3 9 0 9 2 2 3 0 6 2 2 7 9 9 3 8 0
9 0 9 2 3 6 2 5 2 8 6 5 3 9 5 3 4 6 5 0 4 0 7 6 7 8 5 9 9 1 3 2 2 4 2 1 8 7 7 3
2 3 7 8 1 8 6 4 5 1 9 1 5 8 6 2 3 7 1 3 0 8 0 1 0 0 6 0 9 8 1 4 4 0 5 5 8 6 6 0
7 3 4 3 7 1 5 8 8 1 0 2 6 4 2 2 7 5 3 3 8 9 4 5 1 7 8 3 5 5 6 0 8 4 2 1 4 0 9 8
7 3 4 4 7 1 6 5 8 8 9 0 2 6 9 8 2 5 1 5 1 4 9 8 1 0 7 8 8 8 4 1 1 2 9 3 1 3 8 7
2 2 9 6 9 9 1 0 3 5 2 8 5 2 9 6 9 5 4 2 3 9 6 7 1 0 6 0 2 1 5 2 2 2 2 5 7 4 6 5
1 6 2 5 6 4 5 3 6 7 3 5 5 3 4 4 7 5 8 4 0 6 5 5 9 7 7 7 2 8 3 5 4 0 7 3 5 6 3 5
```

TEST 3: Five-minute binary numbers

You have 5 minutes to memorize binaries, row by row. Score a point for every binary in the correct position (maximum 750). Deduct 15 digits for one mistake in a row; deduct 30 digits for two or more mistakes. A score of 30–60 is good; more than 60 is excellent. The World Record is 870.

1 1 1 0 1 1 1 0 0 1 0 0 1 1 0 0 0 1 0 1 1 0 1 1 1 1 0 1 1 0   Row 1

1 1 0 1 1 1 0 1 1 1 1 1 1 1 1 0 0 1 0 1 0 1 1 1 1 1 0 0 1   Row 2

0 1 0 1 1 0 1 0 0 1 1 1 0 0 1 0 0 1 0 0 0 1 1 0 0 0 1 1 0 0   Row 3

0 0 0 0 1 0 1 1 1 0 0 0 0 1 0 1 0 0 0 1 0 0 1 0 1 1 1 1 0 1   Row 4

0 1 1 1 0 1 1 1 1 1 0 1 0 0 0 0 1 0 1 0 1 1 1 1 0 1 0 0 0 1 1   Row 5

1 1 1 0 0 1 0 1 0 0 0 0 1 0 0 1 0 0 0 1 1 0 0 1 0 1 0 1 1 1   Row 6

1 1 1 1 1 1 1 1 1 1 1 1 0 0 0 0 1 0 1 1 0 1 1 1 1 1 0 0 0 0   Row 7

1 0 1 0 0 1 1 0 0 1 1 1 0 1 0 1 1 0 0 0 1 1 1 1 1 0 0 0 1 0   Row 8

0 1 1 0 0 1 0 1 0 1 0 0 0 1 1 1 0 0 0 1 1 0 1 0 0 0 1 0 1 1   Row 9

1 0 1 1 0 0 1 1 1 0 0 0 0 1 0 1 1 0 0 0 1 0 1 0 0 0 0 1 0   Row 10

1 0 0 1 1 1 0 0 0 0 0 1 1 1 0 0 1 1 0 0 1 1 1 1 1 0 1 0 1 0   Row 11

1 1 0 0 1 0 1 0 1 1 0 0 1 0 1 0 1 1 0 1 0 1 1 0 0 0 0 1 1 0   Row 12

1 0 1 0 1 1 0 0 1 0 0 1 0 0 0 1 1 0 1 1 0 0 0 1 1 1 1 1 0 0   Row 13

0 1 0 1 0 0 0 1 1 0 1 1 1 1 1 0 1 1 1 1 0 0 1 1 1 1 1 1 0 0   Row 14

1 1 1 1 0 1 1 0 0 1 1 0 1 1 0 1 0 0 0 1 1 1 1 1 1 0 1 1 1 1   Row 15

1 1 1 0 1 0 1 0 0 0 1 0 0 0 0 1 1 0 0 1 1 1 1 0 1 0 1 1 0 0   Row 16

0 0 0 1 1 1 0 0 0 0 0 1 1 1 0 1 0 0 0 0 0 0 1 1 1 1 1 0 0 0   Row 17

1 0 0 1 0 1 1 1 1 0 0 0 0 0 1 1 1 0 0 0 0 0 1 1 1 1 1 0 0 1   Row 18

0 0 0 1 1 0 0 1 0 1 0 1 1 1 0 1 1 0 0 1 1 1 0 0 1 0 1 0 1 1   Row 19

0 0 0 0 0 1 1 0 0 1 1 0 1 0 0 0 0 0 0 0 0 1 0 1 1 1 0 0 1   Row 20

0 0 0 1 1 1 1 1 1 0 1 1 0 0 1 0 0 0 0 0 1 1 0 0 1 1 1 0 1   Row 21

0 1 0 0 1 0 1 0 0 0 0 0 1 0 1 0 0 1 1 0 1 1 0 0 0 0 1 0 1 1   Row 22

1 0 0 1 1 0 1 0 0 1 1 0 1 0 0 1 1 1 0 1 1 0 1 1 1 1 0 1 1 0   Row 23

1 0 1 1 0 1 0 0 0 1 1 0 1 1 0 0 1 0 0 0 1 0 0 1 1 1 1 1 1 1   Row 24

0 1 0 0 0 1 0 0 1 0 1 1 1 1 0 1 1 0 0 0 1 0 1 0 1 1 0 1 0 1   Row 25

AFTERWORD: THE CHAMPIONS OF THE FUTURE

I wanted to end this book with a short note on why I think passing on my techniques for a perfect memory is so important, and why I want you to pass them on, too. When I was at school, nobody showed me how to learn. Like my peers, I was expected to absorb and process knowledge in the best way I could and then regurgitate it in exams to show what had stuck. Looking back, I think I would have performed an awful lot better if someone had given me a few basic tips on memorization.

Today, our children are taught completely differently from the way I was taught then. When I was at school, the emphasis was on learning by rote, and it was all about what we could memorize from a book and then write down in an exam. Now, children are expected to display what they've learned not just by examination, but through projects and hands-on assignments. They have to show that they truly understand what they've been taught.

However, despite these changes, a trained memory continues to provide an invaluable tool for improving understanding. In whatever way they learn, children build every day on the information they learned the day, week, month and year before.

Memory in school is as fundamental today as it has ever been if we want to create a future filled with bright, focused minds that aspire to achieve their full potential.

In 2008, I became involved in taking memory techniques into UK schools. The idea was not to teach memory tricks, but to show students how, by engaging in "games" that use their memory, they could improve their learning. We sent presenters into schools to deliver a two-hour presentation. The students spent the next few weeks practising what they'd been taught by the presentation and then took part in an in-school competition. The format worked: students, teachers and parents alike have all told us that the skills we teach have been easily transferable to actual study. They have seen students achieve academic success, experience improved self-esteem and discover greater motivation to learn and study. The enthusiasm was such that we set up the UK Schools Memory Championships, which now has more than 10,000 participants each year.

What students and their carers – and I – have come to appreciate is that memory training, using the techniques in this book, engages the whole of the brain and not just the functions involved in processing linear information. So, yes, the techniques would have helped me hugely in the days of learning by rote, but they continue to benefit students today because they give so much more than simply an ability to memorize a list of facts. When we use memory techniques, whether we are children or adults, we make links between disparate pieces of information using imaginative, colourful pictures. The techniques stimulate our minds and reveal how memory – and learning – works.

The only dissenting voice I've ever heard about the methods I've suggested to schools was from a teacher who asked me, "What's the point in teaching memory? Learning is not about remembering. It's about understanding." I asked him for one example of anything that he'd understood that did not involve the function of memory. He didn't give me an answer.

Although I don't agree with that teacher, I do understand his unwillingness to be drawn in. What *is* the point in memorizing a 2,000-digit number or 20 shuffled decks of playing cards? But then, what's the point in running around a 400-metre track as fast as you can when all you're really doing is going round in circles? What, indeed, is the point in 11 fully grown men kicking a football from one end of a field to try to get it in a net at the other end, while another 11 fully grown men try to stop them? The point, whether it's football, running, tennis, ice hockey, darts, memory or any game you care to mention, is that the process of getting there, of being successful, involves learning on many levels – learning how to be good at something, learning how to accept failure and push on until you succeed, learning to be proud in your achievements (and gracious in defeat), learning to feel good about yourself.

Field sports exercise your body; learning the order of 52 cards (useless as it might be in itself) exercises your brain. It offers you irrefutable evidence of the limitless capacity of your imagination. When children, or any of us, practise memory training, we unleash our creative thinking. When we begin to push the boundaries of what we thought was possible, and to reveal the true potential of our incredible brains, we experience a surge in

INSIDE MY MIND: KNOWING THAT IT'S WORTH IT

A few years ago, I was invited to give a presentation to children from a number of under-performing schools. I spent three hours with these students, giving them memory demonstrations and getting them to perform a feat of memory themselves. That was the first time I'd taught a group of school children. On my way home, I wondered if it had been a worthwhile exercise. Had I managed to inspire the children, or had I just acted as an interesting diversion? Would the children slip back to their normal ways or had they learned a valuable lesson – a new skill they could nurture to make the job of learning achievable?

Five years later, I was helping to run the UK Open Memory Championships in London when a man tapped me on the shoulder and said, "Mr O'Brien, you won't remember me, but a few years ago when I was a student, I attended your memory skills session." He'd been in that very first group of students. He told me that I'd given him a copy of one of my books. It had taken him a while to settle down to read it, but when he did, everything that I'd taught him that day came back to him and suddenly made perfect sense.

He told me that he'd used the techniques to help him pass his exams and he now had a place at university. When I asked him what he was doing at the competition, he said with a degree of pride that he was a competitor. That year he came eighth and the following year he was the silver medallist, losing only to the World Champion, Ben Pridmore.

If ever I doubt the use of sharing my techniques, I think of this story as affirmation of the benefits of what I do. If it can make a difference to just one child in a class, then every minute spent teaching and sharing what I've learned has been worthwhile.

self-confidence. When children, in particular, discover the power of their memory, they get to the heart of the learning process, and begin to understand that the job of absorbing knowledge can be fun, inspiring and rewarding – not just something that mum, dad and a bunch of teachers say you have to do. Also, with the mounting evidence that training your working memory increases fluid intelligence (the brain functions that allow us to think laterally to solve a problem, without necessarily conforming to predetermined patterns; see pp.190–92), you could say that the teaching of memory skills is a no-brainer.

I hope you've enjoyed your journey with me. Writing this book has taken me through my own personal history with this game of memory, and I hope I've enabled you to see how training your amazing memory can not only bring perfect recall, but so much more besides. Have a look at my timeline on the opposite page to feel inspired. Who knows, perhaps we'll meet at a memory championship in the future? I hope we do!

INSIDE MY MIND: MY MEMORY FEATS TIMELINE

Date	Memory feat
1987	Started memory training; First deck of cards memorized in 26 minutes
1989	World Record: 6 decks of cards
June 11, 1989	World Record: 25 decks of cards
July 22, 1990	World Record: 35 decks of cards
October 26, 1991	World Memory Champion (1st time)
August 8, 1993	World Memory Champion (2nd time)
November 26, 1993	World Record: 40 decks of cards
1994	The Brain Trust's "Brain of The Year"
March 25, 1994	World Record: Speed Cards memorizing 1 deck in 43.59 seconds
1995	Awarded Grandmaster of Memory by HRH Prince Philip of Liechtenstein
April 21, 1995	Won first World Matchplay Championships
August 6, 1995	World Memory Championship (3rd time)
1996	World Record: Speed Cards memorizing 1 deck in 38.29 seconds
August 4, 1996	World Memory Champion (4th time)
August 23, 1997	World Memory Champion (5th time)
August 27, 1999	World Memory Champion (6th time)
August 22, 2000	World Memory Champion (7th time)
2001	World Record: Memorizing 2 decks of cards simultaneously
August 26, 2001	World Memory Champion (8th time)
May 1, 2002	World Record: 54 decks of cards
2005	Lifetime achievement award for promoting memory worldwide, awarded by the World Memory Championships International
2008	Co-founder and Chief Co-ordinator of the Schools Memory Championships
2010	General Manager of the World Memory Sports Council

INDEX